Saint Augustine's Confessions Book 1

Latin Text with Facing Vocabulary and Commentary

Joshua C. Shaw

Saint Augustine's Confessions Book 1
Latin Text with Facing Vocabulary and Commentary

First Edition

Published by JCSTexts

Cover design by Jared Eckert. Email him with questions or design projects at jareddeckert@gmail.com.

The Latin Text was edited by James J. O'Donnell (1992) and initially prepared (though edited by the present author) by Geoffrey Steadman.

ISBN-13: 978-1-7348443-0-6

Table of Contents

Pages

Acknowledgments.....iii

Preface to the Series.....v-vi

Preface to *Confessions* I.....vii-ix

Running Vocabulary.....xi-xiv

Glossary and Resources.....xvi-xviii

Text with Commentary.....1-54

Latin Text for Classroom Use.....55-74

Alphabetized Core Vocabulary List.....75-78

Dictionary of Grammatical Terms.....81-84

Acknowledgments

This project is indebted to a number of people. First thanks goes to Geoffrey Steadman, without whose encouragement and advice I could not have written this. He created the intial text, which I then corrected and outfitted with commentary.[1] In this connection I must also thank Dr. James O'Donnell, who has graciously allowed me to use his text: the fruits of his tireless labor in the study of Augustine's *Confessions*. Truly his commentary is a *magnum opus et arduum*, and I can only hope that this commentary and those to follow bring more grateful readers to his work.

The original inspiration for the work belongs to the course I taught this summer at Hillsdale College: thanks to Joey, Mark, Jose, Griffin, Mike, and Christian for enduring seven long weeks of six-hour daily coursework (and many more hours of study!). A thanks likewise to the professors at Hillsdale College, especially Dr. Garnjobst and Dr. Hutchinson, who together with the Politics department provided me the oppportunity in the first place. Dr. Hutchinson was particularly brave to hazard a raw version of the commentary on another class of students.

To Professor Catherine Conybeare I owe my first introduction to Augustine's *Confessions* and to his Latin in general: her insightful analysis of the same has helped me to see the beauty and magic of Augustine's art.

Finally to the patience and kindness of my wife: I owe a special thanks to you. Few would willingly move four times within the span of a year, not to mention transcontinentally, yet you have done it with grace and energy.

[1] With the exception of *Confessions* VIII I will be producing the texts for all following commentaries myself.

Preface to the Series

> Each author has a grammar of his own, written or unwritten. Each student has a gramar of his own, has his ways of adjusting the phenomena to his range of vision or *vice versa*, less frequently *vice versa.*
>
> Basil Gildersleeve, *Problems in Greek Syntax*

"I confess myself to be among those who write to progress and in progressing write," and grammar notes are no exception. When I articulate to myself the fine distinctions in the text with the help of grammar I finally understand what *I think* the author is saying, against which I can then judge what the *author* is in fact saying. Thus it is often not (merely) the author who is not clear to us, but that we are not clear to ourselves.

For this reason I believe we need to be reminded of the basics, e.g., anaphora, inner and outer accusatives, ablative (or genitive, as the case may be) absolutes, and the vexing problems of syntax in indirect discourse. There is much to be said for crawling before walking and walking before running--yet here is the difficulty. The basis for appreciating a literary text is an underlying enjoyment of the matter at hand. But, *at least for a while*, the searching of commentaries and grammars and lexica dampens this joy for many, however surely it leads to greater joy in the end. And so the very means of greater enjoyment of the text are themselves instruments of tedium in the extreme: what is the student to do?

Faced with this dilemma students will find this type of commentary, i.e., a commentary like those of Steadman and Pharr, a very helpful place to begin. By appending vocabularly and grammar to the text, the commentary maximizes time spent on the text itself and delays for a later time the jarring fragmentation of the text that happens when the reader must spend 30 minutes in between each sentence in grammars and commentaries. Again, while such deep study ought to lead back around to deeper and more satisfying enjoyment of the text in the end, this is hard to perceive in the beginning, and for those who simply do not have those hours in the day, such a commentary allows a glimpse of the goal. I am convinced that this is the way to persuade new students of the language, especially when starting late, that such study is worth their time in the first place.

Perhaps one last word on the utility of attention to grammar is justified. Augustine was, after all, more keenly aware than most of the painful split of I and the Other wrought by the Fall, his *Confessions* is conscious of the immense, but oft-overlooked, trouble of meaningful communication.[1] Keen attention to grammar helps us to transcend the commonest barriers of communication, the abysses dug by time, place, religion, and all those things that constitute our particular culture(s). Writing this commentary has revealed to me more than I knew before of this chasm, and to weary the reader with another quote of Gildersleeve, "at least whole grammars have been constructed about one emptiness."

[1] He hoped that one day we would merely transfer our thoughts from one bosom to the next without the help of language. *Conf.* 11.3.5

Preface to *Confessions* Book I

> confessionum mearum libri tredecim et de malis et de bonis meis deum laudant iustum et bonum atque in eum excitant humanum intellectum et affectum. interim quod ad me attinet, hoc in me egerunt cum scriberentur et agunt cum leguntur. quid de illis alii sentiant, ipsi viderint; multis tamen fratribus eos multum placuisse et placere scio.[1]
>
> *Retractationes*. 2.6.

It is hard to imagine a genre other than the Psalms of David sufficiently pliant and supple to hold the vast heart of Augustine's *Confessions*. The Psalms, at least as much as any other genre of ancient poetry, ranged the multi-textured terrain of human experience: love and hate, sin and redemption, life and death, praise and lament, philosophical wonder and theological delight. But as Professor Conybeare notes in her introduction to the *Confessions*, no one would mistake the *Confessions* for one of David's Psalms.[2] If however Augustine confessed in order to "praise a God just and good" concerning his "evils and goods" and to "rouse to Him (God) the human mind and heart," it is hard to call them anything other than an act of worship. That is, after all, what a confession is.[3]

Would someone confuse the *Confessions* with a Psalm of *David*? I think we can reasonably conclude no. But we would misapprehend the nature of the *Confessions* if we did not recognize them as the Psalms of *Augustine*.[4] They are all together an act of worship, or better, a song of worship, which is at once—through publication—

[1] *The thirteen Books of my confessions praise God both concerning my evils and my goods—a God who is just and good and rouse to him the human mind and heart. In any case so far as concerns me: they did this while they were being written and they do it while they are being read. Let others see for themselves what they think about them; I know that they have pleased many brothers at least and still do.* (Transl. mine; intentionally over-literal)

[2] Page 27 in Catherine Conybeare, *the Routledge GuideBook to the Confessions*, Routledge, 2016.

[3] Ibid. p. 1-2

[4] Given that the unity (and sole authorship) of a multitude of the Psalms is hotly debated, it should come as no surprise that the unity and design of Augustine's Psalm(s) should thus be the center of a long debate. Conybeare (2016) and O'Donnell (1992) give excellent summaries and references to this scholarly debate.

unashamedly public and—through the intimate participation of the reader in Augustine's inner world—blushingly personal. This from a man who wrote the longest sustained commentary in Latin antiquity on the *Psalms*, a book in which public and private worship are inextricably tangled, should not surprise us.

Turning from the whole to the part, we find in Book I the simple yet singular poetry of prayer (i.e., the Psalms). Much in *Confessions* Book I is thus naturally enigmatic: who is the *praedicans* in the first paragraph? what does the *nesciens* in the first paragraph not know and so therefore call on the wrong god? what is the earth and what are the waves to which Monica entrusted Augustine?[5] Augustine the baby is an image pregnant with many fruitful themes and questions for Augustine the man: patterns for thinking about language, memory, time, creation, and divine providence are laid in the infancy of the *Confessions*. A careful study of Book I therefore lays the best groundwork for a sound understanding of the whole.

But perhaps, given that *Confessions* are Augustine's Psalms, and Book I in a way the most psalm-like of all, the question arises, "What claim does the *Confessions* make on the non-Christian?" The first and easiest answer is, the same claim made by Plato on all non-Platonists, by Seneca on non-Stoics, and by Confucius on non-Confucianists, namely, that there exist truths about the world and the human soul and we should pay attention to their answers. We all give ourselves answers to these questions, wittingly or no, and we read these great works of human literature and philosophy to deepen our

[5] You can see the resumption of these ideas later in the *Confessions* at many places, e.g., 5.7.12; 5.13.23; 6.1.1; for the water as sin and land as the new man book 13.13

reflection on the same and to challenge ourselves in our own thinking about the highest things.

Augustine's idea of originality and quotation might appear equaly strange to a first-time reader of the *Confessions*: "why are the *Confessions* replete with quotations of Scripture?" The answer is simple and might be best illustrated by example: the ancients, or in this case, at least Augustine, simply did not find it inconsistent to give voice to one's deepest emotions through the words of another, witness Christ's words on the cross.[6] Beyond the Christian world it is well known that the expression of the self through the (authoritative) words of another was taught in the secular schools of rhetoric.[7] Suffice it to say, the question of originality in the ancient world balanced itself on different axes than the modern counterpart.

A last note is that Augustine's remarks in the *Reconsiderations* end on pleasure: the *Confessions* "have pleased some brothers and still do." The *Confessions* were written to please. From the smallest points of grammar and style (why does he use *ego* here and not *sum* and *vice versa*), to the problems of paradox (*quoniam loquaces muti sunt*), to the startling uses of metaphor (*in quorum et ego auribus parturiebam quidquid sentiebam*), "the way forward for students of the *Confessions* lies in renewed and assiduous attention to the most minute details of the text" and in this attention to *enjoy it.*[8]

---

[6] For this point it is irrelevant whether Christ said the words of the 22nd Psalm or not ('my God my God why have you forsaken me?'), for it is clear that the writer and audience found them unproblematic—at least so far as we can see from the text and responses to it.

[7] Cf. Boissier in Gibbs and Montgomery's commentary on 1.17.27: "The pressure which compells [the student] to make a speech in the name of another wakens and opens the spirit [of the student] and so it happens that he learns to discern his own feelings in attempting to express those of a stranger." Along a similar line see also vol. 2 p. 91 of O'Donnell's Commentary.

[8] O'Donnel, *Vol. 1: Text and Introduction*, lxii.

RUNNING CORE VOCABULARY CONFESSIONS BOOK I

Below are given all words in Book I of the Confessions occurring 5 or more times in the order in which they occur. The numbers to the left correspond to the pages and those on the right to the number of times which they occur. An alphabetized version of this list is given for the convenience of the reader at the end of the commentary.

1 **ad**: to, toward, 26
1 **aliquis, aliquid (quī, quid)**: anyone, anything; some, any, 19
1 **alius, -a, -ud**: other, another, else, 19
1 **an**: or (in questions), 20
1 **cor, cordis n.** heart,
1 **dēlectō (1)**: delight (compl. inf.), please, in pass. + abl. 5
1 **dō, dare, dedī, datum**: give; grant, 22
1 **dominus, -ī m.**: master, lord, 44
1 **ego, mihi, mē, mē**: I, 142
1 **enim**: for, indeed, in truth, 46
1 **et**: and; also, even, 315
1 **faciō, -ere, fēcī, factum**: do, make, 40
1 **homō, -inis m./f.**: man, mortal, human, 32
1 **in**: in (+ abl.) , into (acc.), 111
1 **invocō (1)**: call on, pray to, invoke, 15
1 **laudō (1)**: praise, glorify, 11
1 **magnus, -a, -um**: great, large; important, 9
1 **nesciō, -īre, -scīvī, -scītum**: not know, 9
1 **nōn**: not, 117
1 **nōs, nōbīs**: we, us, 18
1 **noster, nostra, nostrum**: our, 13
1 **peccātum, -ī n.**: sin, offense, 10
1 **possum, posse, potuī**: be able, can, avail, 18
1 **potius**: rather, preferably (comp. of *potis* 'possible'), 6
1 **prō**: before, for, in behalf of; in accordance with (abl.), 6
1 **quī, quae, quod (quis? quid?)**: who, which, that, 211
1 **quia**: because, that 25
1 **sciō, -īre, -īvī (iī), -ītus**: know (how + inf.), 8
1 **sed**: but, 38
1 **sum, esse, fuī, futūrum**: be, 164
1 **suus, -a, -um**: his, her, its, their (own), 16
1 **tamen**: nevertheless, however, anyway22
1 **tū**: you, 136
1 **tuus, -a, -um**: your, yours, 55
1 **ut**: as, just as, when (+ ind.); (so) that, in order that, 45
1 **volō, velle, voluī**: will, wish, be willing, (compl. inf.) 20
2 **aut**: or (aut...aut – either…or), 21
2 **autem**: however, but; moreover, 18
2 **crēdō, -ere, -didī, creditum**: believe, trust (+dat.), 11
2 **cum**: with (abl.); when, since, although, 34

2 **deus, -ī m.**: god, divinity, deity, 55

2 **fīlius, -iī m.**: son, 6

2 **inveniō, -īre, -vēnī**: come upon, find, 9

2 **ipse, ipsa, ipsum**: -self; the very, 31

2 **is, ea, id**: this, that; he, she, it, 71

2 **meus, -a, -um**: my, mine, 122

2 **per**: through, over, across (acc), 22

2 **quaerō, -ere, quaesīvī**: search for, ask, 11

2 **quam**: than, as; how, 32

2 **quoniam**: since now, seeing that, 15

2 **sine**: without (abl.), 9

2 **utique**: in any case, by all means, certainly, 7

2 **veniō, -īre, vēnī, ventus**: come, go, 11

3 **caelum, -ī n.**: sky, heaven, 10

3 **capiō, -ere, cēpī, captum**: take, seize, hold, contain, 10

3 **ergō**: therefore, 17

3 **etiam**: also, even; besides, 24

3 **ē, ex**: out from, from, out of (+ abl.), 16

3 **fiō, fierī, factus sum**: become, be made, happen (+ ut and subj.), 7

3 **iam**: now, already; + nōn, no longer, 20

3 **ita**: so, thus, 18

3 **nam**: for, because, 18

3 **nisi**: if not, unless, except, 18

3 **omnis, omne**: every, all, 43

3 **quisquam, quidquam (quicquam)**: anyone, anything, 14

3 **quisquis, quidquid**: whoever, whatever, 6

3 **sīc**: thus, in this way, 8

3 **terra, -ae. f.**: earth, ground, land; pl. the earth 13

3 **unde**: from where, whence, 7

3 **vērō**: in truth, in fact, certainly, 11

4 **dīcō, -ere, dīxī, dictus**: say, speak, tell, 35

4 **habeō, -ēre, habuī, -itus**: have, hold; consider 13

4 **impleō, -ēre, -ēvī**: fill; fulfill, complete, 11

4 **nec**: and not (nec…nec: neither…nor), 19

4 **tōtus -a, -um**: whole, entire, 5

5 **īdem, eadem, idem**: the same, 6

5 **maior, māius**: greater; older; ancestors, 18

5 **minor, minus**: less, smaller; *adv.* less, 9

5 **ne**: (introduces a yes/no question), 12

5 **nūllus, -a, -um**: none, no, no one, 6

5 **numquam**: never, at no time, 6

5 **rēs, reī, f.**: thing, matter, affair; pl. reality, the universe, 14

5 **rogō (1)**: ask, 5

5 **summus, -a, -um**: highest, greatest, top of, 5

RUNNING CORE VOCABULARY CONFESSIONS BOOK I

6 **agō, -ere, ēgī, āctum**: drive, do, spend, lead (a life), 10
6 **amō (1)**: love, like, 11
6 **nihil**: nothing, 5
6 **vīta, -ae, f.**: life, 13
7 **ā, ab, abs**: (away) from, out of; by, 52
7 **anima, -ae f.**: breath, spirit, soul, 11
7 **ante**: before, in front of (acc.), 7
7 **audiō, -īre, -īvī, audītum**: hear, listen to, 6
7 **auris, auris f.**: ear, 5
7 **bonus, -a, -um**: good, noble, kind, 16
7 **dē**: down from, from, about, concerning (abl), 25
7 **ecce**: behold, look, 8
7 **ille, illa, illud**: that, those, 49
7 **iubeō, iubēre, iussī, iussum**: order, 5
7 **loquor, loquī, locūtus sum**: speak, address, 10
7 **malus, -a, -um**: bad, evil, 5
7 **oblīvīscor, -ī, -lītus sum**: forget (acc. or gen.), 5
7 **parvus, -a, -um**: small, little, 7
7 **peccō (1)**: sin, commit an offense, 8
7 **salūs, -ūtis f.**: safety, refuge; health; salvation 7
7 **sī**: if, 24
7 **ūnus, -a, -um**: one, 7
8 **clāmō (1)**: shout, cry out, 6
8 **hic, haec, hoc**: this, these, 57
8 **morior, morī, mortuus sum**: die, 6
8 **nē**: lest, that not, no, not, 10
8 **nōlō, nōlle, nōluī**: not wish, be unwilling, 7
8 **oculus, -ī, m.**: eye, 5
8 **post**: after, behind (acc.), in A., toward; *adv.* afterward, 6
8 **videō, vidēre, vīdī, vīsum**: see, 20
8 **vōx, vōcis, f.**: sound, voice; word, utterance, quotation 5
9 **fallō, -ere, fefellī, falsum**: deceive, 6
9 **iste, ista, istud**: this/these *or* that/those, 21
9 **parēns, -rentis m.**: parent, ancestor, 7
9 **sē, sibi**: himself, her-, it-, them-, 14
10 **affectus, -ūs m.**: affection, feeling, 6
10 **īnfantia, -ae f.**: inability to speak, infancy, 9
10 **māter, mātris f.**: mother, 11
10 **meminī, -isse**: remember; recall, 6
10 **vel**: or, either…or (inclusive), 16
11 **fleō, -ēre, -ēvī, flētum**: weep, cry, bewail (acc.), 7
11 **īnfāns, -fantis m. f.**: infant, 6
11 **membrum, -ī n.**: limb, member, 5
11 **prīmus -a -um**: first, 5

11 **sēnsus, -ūs m.**: feeling, perception, sensation, 5
11 **sentiō, -īre, sēnsī, sēnsum**: feel, perceive, 5
11 **signum, -ī n.**: sign, signal; symbol, 8
11 **tunc**: then, at that time, 8
11 **ubi**: where, when, 9
11 **voluntās, -tātis f.**: will, wish, desire, 6
12 **discō, -ere, didicī**: learn, come to know, get acquainted with (acc.), 28
12 **magis**: more, rather, 8
12 **que**: and, 18
12 **serviō, -īre, -īvī, -ītum**: be slave to, serve, (dat.), 5
12 **tālis, -e**: of such a sort, 14
12 **vērus, -a, -um**: true, real, 7
13 **aetās, aetātis f.**: age, lifetime, time, 5
13 **miser, -a, -um**: sad, miserable, gloomy, 6
13 **pater, patris, m.**: father, 5
13 **vīvō, -ere, vīxī, vīctum**: live, 12
14 **atque (=ac)**: and, and also, and even, 24
14 **cōnfiteor, -ērī, -fessum**: admit, reveal, confess (dat.) 7
14 **multus, -a, -um**: much, many, 9
15 **adhūc**: thus, to this point, still; even, just, 5
15 **diēs, -ēī m./f.**: day, time, season, 5
15 **modus, -ī m.**: way, manner; limit; just, only, 5
15 **trānseō, -īre, -iī (īvī), itus**: pass (by), 6
15 **via, -ae, f.**: way, road, street, 6
16 **nunc**: now, at present, 6
16 **reprehendō, -ere, -dī**: blame; hold back; scold, 5
17 **animus, -ī m**: soul, will; minī; intention, 7
18 **nōndum**: not yet, 5
20 **puer, puerī, m.**: boy, 20
21 **littera, -ae f.**: letter (of the alphabet); pl. literature, epistle, 12
21 **verbum, -ī n.**: word, speech, 16
22 **vultus, -ūs m.**: expression, countenance, face, 5
23 **cōgō, -ere, -ēgī, coactum**: compel; 6
23 **prōpōnō, -ere, -suī, -situm**: put or set forth, 5
25 **legō, -ere, lēgī, lectum**: read, choose, 9
25 **magister, magistrī m.**: teacher, 7
25 **scrībō, -ere, scrīpsī, scrīptum**: write, 11
26 **lūdō, -ere, lūsī, lūsus**: play; play with, 5
27 **bene**: well, 8
27 **melior, melius**: better, 6
29 **quasi**: as if, 6
32 **error errōris m.**: wandering, error, 8
32 **ōdī, -isse**: hate, 5
32 **urgeō, -ere, ursī**: press, urge, distress, 5

33 **Graecus, -a, -um**: Greek, 5

33 **grammaticus, -a, -um.**: of grammar, grammatical; *m. subst.* grammarian, teacher of the second level of education in the Roman world, after students had learned their ABC's, 5

34 **Aenēās, -ae m.**: Aeneas, 5

38 **vānus, -a, -um**: worthless; vain, futile, false, 5

40 **lēx, lēgis f.**: law, regulation, decree, 7

Glossary[1]

abs.	absolute	impf.	imperfect
acc.	accusative	ind	indirect
act.	active	indic.	indicative
adj.	adjective	indir. comm.	Indirect Command
adv.	adverb	indir. qu	Indirect Question
ag.	agent	inf.	infinitive
antec.	antecedent	inter.	interrogative
apod.	apodosis	l./ln.	line
app.	appositive	m.	masculine
circums.	circumstantial	n.	neuter
CL	Classical Latin	nom.	nominative
cl.	clause	obj.	object
char.	characteristic	p./pg.	page
comp.	comparative	pl.	plural
comp.	compound	pple.	participle
concess.	concessive	pass	passive
cond.	condition(al)	pf.	perfect
conn. rel.	connective relative	ppp	pf. pass. part.
CTF	Contrary to Fact	pers.	person
dat.	dative	plfpf.	pluperfect
dep.	deponent	pred.	predicate
dir.	direct	pr.	present
disc.	discourse	prim.	primary
expl.	explanation	prot.	protasis
f.	feminine	rel.	relative
FLV	Future Less Vivid	s/sg.	singular
FMV	Future More Vivid	seq.	sequence
FMtV	Future Most Vivid	subj.	subject
fut.	future	subj.	subjunctive
gen.	genitive	subst.	substantive
gen.	general	superl.	superlative
imper.	imperative	v.	verb
IL	Imperial Latin	voc.	vocative
impers.	impersonal		

The text: The text used in this edition is that of Dr. James O'Donnell (1992 and see below), who maintained the traditional division into chapters (from Amerbach's ed. in 1506) and paragraphs (from the Maurist eds. in the 1800's). Both are used in citations of the *Confessions*. The only change I have made to O'Donnell's text is to use the Benedictine reading at 1.14.23 in place of O'Donnell's crux. Otherwise (with the edition of macrons) the text is the same as his.

[1] For the convenience of the reader, I have made a dictionary of grammatical and rhetorical terms, to be found at the end of the work in alphabetical order.

Using this Commentary

Before proceeding to the actual text, it is suggested that the student look over the running vocabulary, where all words occurring five times or more in Book I of the *Confessions* are given in the order in which they occur. Once done, this will allow the student to focus on the words on the page without consulting (at first) additional grammars, lexica, or commentaries. While reading, try to read whole sentences without help: aloud, if possible. Make guesses and take away the main idea. Then return to the beginning of the sentence and with the help of the vocabulary and notes work through every form and tough bit of syntax. If at this point more depth (or review) is desired, the reader is given references to Allen and Greenough as well as Cambell and McGuire (about which see below).[2] It is of course wished that the student consult (often) the commentaries of Clark and O'Donnell. Because the commentary of Gibbs and Montgomery is far less accessible than the others, and because many comments contain notes or parallel passages in other languages, I have taken what I thought the best of these comments and translated them for the reader. For the sake of space, I have not given specific references to the works of Augustine or other authors but instead have simply marked them with "G&M". Should the reader want the precise references he or she can easily find them in the respective commentaries at the relevant lemmas. For additional helpful tips for reading Latin and Greek or using commentaries like this one, see Geoffrey Steadman's introductions to his commentaries and his page "Habits Matter" on his website (geoffreysteadman.com).

[2] I should also note here that I have given broad generalizations about Classical, Imperial (and rarely Late) Latin: I have not used these terms with great strictness. They are merely guidelines for the beginning student: it is hoped that, should the student want to know more about the progress of Latin language, he or she will look into the authorities on that subject--this task being of course beyond the scope of an introductory textbook like this one.

Further Resources[3]

(*those cited in the commentary are preceded by the corresponding abbreviation*)

A&G	Allen and Greenough's *New Latin Grammar*, 1903 Revision.[4]
Arts	Arts, Mary. *The Syntax of the Confessions of Saint Augustine*, Diss. CUA, Washington DC, 1927.[5]
	Brown, Peter, *Augustine of Hippo, a Biography*. Oxford Univeristy Press, 1967.[6]
C&M	Cambell and McGuire's Introduction to their *Selections*.
Clark	Clark, Gillian, *Confessions* Books I-IV, Cambridge Greek and Latin Classics, 1995.
	Conybeare, Catherine, *The Routledge Guidebook to Augustine's Confessions*. Routledge Press, 2016.[7]
G&M	Gibb and Montgomery. *Confessionum libri XIII*. 2nd ed., Cambridge, 1927.
G&L	Gildersleeve and Lodge's Latin Grammar (1903 Ed.)[8]
	Hrdlicka, Clement. *A Study of the Late Latin Vocabulary and of the Prepostions and Demonstrative Pronouns in the Confessions*. Diss. CUA, Washington DC, 1931.[9]
L&S	Lewis and Short's Latin Dictionary.[10]
O'Donnell	O'Donnel, James, Confessions: *Text and Commentary*, 3 vols. Oxford University Press, 1992.[11]
TLL	*Thesaurus Linguae Latinae*. Bayerische Akademie der Wissenschaften.[12]

[3] The reader is also encouraged to make use of *Latinperdiem* videos on youtube: an excellent resource in general and one of the only (accessible) resoucres for Latin written after the Imperial Period. He has, I believe, covered most of book I of the *Confessions*; if therefore my notes are not enough, this resource is a good next step.

[4] Available for free through perseus.tufts.edu.

[5] Though I have found it at some points dated or inexhaustive, it is nevertheless a useful overview to the syntax of the *Confessions*, if something more thorough than Cambell and McGuire is wished. As is the case to a lesser degree in Hrdlicka, Art in essence applies the findings of the most authoritateive (often German) grammars which include late Latin to the text of the *Confessions*.

[6] Has been, still is, and will likely remain the standard treatment for a long time to come.

[7] An up-to-date and fresh introduction to Augustine's *Confessions*, where one can find great summaries of scholarship as well as the author's own insightful views.

[8] Used often but cited rarely for the mere fact that it is less used in Latin classrooms today. Nevertheless it is available online through perseus.tufts.edu and is a superb resource: generally more reliable than A&G for more advanced questions of syntax and usage diachronically.

[9] Rather more exhaustive use of the TLL is made in this dissertation than that of Arts and is therefore on the whole more reliable. However, it is likely far more than the average beginning student of the *Confessions* desires. Nevertheless, if a better answer is sought on the use of a particular preposition or demonstrative this is still a very useful resources.

[10] available online at perseus.tufts.edu

[11] *An absolutely indispensable aid to a deep understanding of the Confessions, happily (and generously) available online to all via or stoa.org/hippo*

[12] The most comphrensive dictionary of Latin, available online at thesaurus.badw.de. An import resource for the thinly-resourced world of late antique Latin.

Through daily chatter words have become cheap to us, because in being noised and in passing us by words become cheap and they seem to be nothing other than words.
Augustine

The way forward for students of the *Confessions* lies in renewed and assiduous attention to the most minute details of the text.
James O'Donnell

Magnum opus omnino et arduum conamur; sed nihil difficile amanti puto.
Cicero

Confessionum Liber I

1.1.1 magnus es, domine, et laudābilis valdē. magna virtūs tua et sapientiae tuae nōn est numerus. et laudāre tē vult homō, aliqua portiō creātūrae tuae, et homō circumferēns mortālitātem suam, circumferēns testimōnium peccātī suī et testimōnium quia superbīs resistis; et tamen laudāre tē vult homō, aliqua portiō creātūrae tuae. tū excitās ut laudāre tē dēlectet, quia fēcistī nōs ad tē et inquiētum est cor nostrum dōnec requiēscat in tē. dā mihi, domine, scīre et intellegere utrum sit prius invocāre tē an laudāre tē, et scīre tē prius sit an invocāre tē. sed quis tē invocat nesciēns tē? aliud enim prō aliō potest invocāre nesciēns. an potius invocāris ut sciāris?

---

circumferō, -ferre, -tulī: carry around (with one), make known, flaunt (TLL A.3, C.1), 2
creātūra, -ae f.: creation, creature, 3
dōnec: until
excitō (1): wake, rouse, call on
inquiētus, -a, -um: restless, disturbed; disquieting 2
intellegō, -ere, -lēxī, -lēctum: realize, understand, 4
laudābilis, -e: worthy of praise, laudable, 3
mortālitās, -ātis f.: mortality
numerus, -ī m.: number, count, multitude, 2
portiō, -iōnis f.: portion, part, section, 2
prior, prius: before, earlier (comp. prīmus), 4
requiēscō, -ere, requiēvī: rest
resistō, -ere, -stitī: resist, oppose (dat) 2
sapientia, -ae f.: wisdom
superbus, -a, -um: arrogant, proud, 3
testimonium, -iī n.; evidence, witness, 2
utrum: whether (often with *an*, 'or') 4
valdē: very, very much; *comp.* valdius
virtūs, -ūtis f.: strength, *power*, virtue, 2

1 **et**: in the *C*, particularly in prayers, *et* often has the force of *sed, cum,* or even *si*, connected by Augustine with biblical language in an attempt to "restore integrity to language" (O'Donnell).
2 **sapientiae...numerus**: *a counting (limit) of your wisdom*; obj. gen.
3 **circumferēns**: m. nom. sg. pres. act. concess. part. as a counterpoint to **tamen**
4 **quia... resistis**: *that you resist the proud*; In CL one would find an expl. *ut*-clause w/ subj. following an adj. or, as here, a noun (A&G 570, 571.c)
superbis: dat. with special verb (A&G 367)
6 **excitas (eum) ut... delectet**: 3 sg. pres. act. subj. in purp. clause. (A&G 531.1)
laudāre... delectet: *...may delight... to praise*: *delectō* was generally used impersonally in CL with the acc. or else in the pass. + inf.
7 **donec requiescat**: *till it rests*; *dum* and **donec** take subj. when suspense or intention are implied (A&G 553 n.1)
da mihi...scire...intellegere: *dare* + dat. and inf. means to allow someone to do something. (A&G 460.a)
8 **utrum sit...an...sit**: *whether.. or..* subjs. in indir. ques.
invocare... laudare... scire... invocare: subj. infins.
prius: we would expect *quam* instead of **an** in normal prose (A&G 434). This effects a kind of halting (not flowing) rhythm as well as something of suspense.
9 **nesciens**: nom. m. s. pr. act. part.
10 **ut sciaris**: *so that you may be known*; 2 sing. pres. pass. subj. (A&G 531.1)
aliud... nesciens: *since he is ignorant*; m. nom. sg. pr. act. caus. part.
potest: *might*; Latin sometimes uses the indic. to express possibility when English would use the subj. (A&G 437.a)

quōmodo autem invocābunt, in quem nōn crēdidērunt? aut quōmodo crēdent sine praedicante? et laudābunt dominum quī requīrunt eum: quaerentēs enim inveniunt eum et invenientēs laudābunt eum. quaeram tē, domine, invocāns tē et invocem tē crēdēns in tē: praedicātus enim es nōbīs. invocat tē, domine, fidēs mea, quam dedistī mihi, quam īnspīrāstī mihi per hūmānitātem fīliī tuī, per ministerium praedicātōris tuī.

1.2.2 et quōmodo invocābō deum meum, deum et dominum meum, quoniam ūtique in mē ipsum eum vocābō, cum invocābō eum? et quis locus est in mē quō veniat in mē deus meus, quō deus

---

fīdēs, eī f.: faith; trust, loyalty, 3
hūmānitās, -tātis f.: culture, *humanity*, 1
īnspīrō (1): breathe into, 1
locus -ī m. (pl. loca): place, region, 4
ministerium, -ī n.: office; service, ministry, 1
praedicātor, -ōris m.: preacher, proclaimer, 1
praedico (1): proclaim, extol, *preach* 2
quōmodo: how, in what way, 4
requīrō, -ere: seek out, ask, inquire, 2
vocō (1): call, summon, 4

11 **(eī) invocābunt (eum)...**
in quem nōn crēdidērunt: in CL we would have *crēdere* + dat. (C&M 88.3)
12 **praedicante:** *a preacher lit. a man preaching*; m. abl. sg. pr. act. subst. part.; parts. often have –e in abl. when subst. and –i when a proper adj. (A&G 119).
13 **quaerentēs...invenientēs:** *if they seek... if they find...*; nom. m. pl. pr. act. cond. parts.
14 **quaeram... invocem:** *let me seek... invoke*; 1 s. pr. act. hort. subjs.
15 **praedicatus es:** *you were preached to us*; notice the ring composition: A. begins by noting how man carries around the *testimonium peccati sui*, but ends the paragraph with God's heralding the promise of forgiveness, grasped by *fides*.
16 **īnspīrā(vi)stī:** 2 sg. pf. act. ind. syncopation of pf. (A&G 181).
fidēs ... quam īnspīrāstī mihi: *the faith which you breathed into me*; as in Gen. 2.7 whence A. took the grammar (C&M 82). Takes the dat. here by analogy to compounds with in- which take the dat. (A&G 370a). **quam** is here the inner object (i.e., not separable from the act of breathing, since the breath itself *is* the life. A&G 390)
quam... quam... per... per: chiasmus
per hūmānitātem... per ministerium: CL more often has *a/ab* + abl. instead of instrumental *per* + acc. (C&M 86c)
17 **praedicatoris tui:** some interpret as Ambrose, but A.'s intention in this introduction is to universalize his experience, to which the use of the passive (*praedicatus*) and the substantive participle (*praedicante*) attest. There is thus an emphasis on God's agency instead of any one person.
18 **meum:** = **deum possidere;** *to possess God* (G&M).
19 **ūtique:** *certainly, in any case*; a limiting particle of confirmation, like *certē* or *saltem.*
invocabo...in...vocabo etc.: *how will I call on him since I will call him on in to me when I call on him?*; a rare case of tmesis ("splitting" of prefix and verb stem) in prose. A.'s concern for the spatial location of God turns our attention to his Manicheaen roots. "The Divine immanence, he holds, is dynamic, not local" (G&M)
20 **quo veniat:** *to which he can come*; rel. cl. of ch. in prim. seq. (A&G 535.1)

veniat in mē, deus quī fēcit caelum et terram? itane, domine deus meus? est quicquam in mē quod capiat tē? an vērō caelum et terra, quae fēcistī et in quibus mē fēcistī, capiunt tē? an quia sine tē nōn esset quidquid est, fit ut quidquid est capiat tē? quoniam itaque et ego sum, quid petō ut veniās in mē, quī nōn essem nisi essēs in mē? nōn enim ego iam īnferī, et tamen etiam ibi es, nam etsī dēscenderō in īnfernum, ades. nōn ergō essem, deus meus, nōn omnīnō essem, nisi essēs in mē. an potius nōn essem nisi essem in tē, ex quō omnia, per quem omnia, in quō omnia? etiam sīc, domine, etiam sīc. quō tē invocō, cum in tē sim? aut unde veniās in

---

adsum, -esse, -fuī: be present/at hand
dēscendō, -ere, -ndī, -nsum: descend, 2
etsī: although, even if, 2
ibi: there, in that place, 2
īnfernum, ī n. (-us, -ī m.): place below, underworld, hell, 1
īnferus, -a, -um: lower, below; pl. subst. underworld, *Hades*, 1
itaque: and so, 4
omnīnō: altogether, (strengthens neg.) *at all* 4
petō, -ere, -īvī, -ītum: seek, head for, *ask*, 3

21 **itane... an... an...:** enclitic *-ne* introduces a question and *an* continues it. (A&G 335)
caelum et terram: in Genesis short for 'the cosmos'. (O'Donnel)

22 **meus:** in CL we would have *mī.* Through Latin translations of the Bible, A. inherits a tendency to use adjs. in the nom. with a noun in the voc.
quod capiat: *which could hold you.* rel. cl. of char. in prim. seq. (A&G 535.a) Normally rel. cl. of char. with indefinite antecedents can be translated indicatively, but here A. seems to be considering the ability or possibility of something in himself 'containing God' and hence *could.*

23 **(quidquid est) non esset:** *whatever is would not be*; apod. of pr. CTF. cond. (A&G 517) The prot. is suppressed: **sine te** = *nisi esses.*

24 **fit ut...capiat:** *(does it) happen that*; verbs of causing and happening often take an ut noun-clause whose verb is in the subj. (A&G 569.2)
quidquid est... quidquid est: subjs. of **esset** and **capiat** respectively.

25 **et ego sum:** *I too exist*
quid petō ut veniās...: *why do I ask that you come...*; an *ut* noun-clause following verbs of will and desire (indir. comm.) takes the subj. Translate as indic. (A&G 563)
(ego) quī nōn essem nisi essēs : *I who would not exist unless you were existing (too)* pr. CTF cond. (A&G 517)

26 **non... īnferī**: *I no longer belong to Hades*; poss. gen. or nom. pl. *I am no longer hell.* Fuller discussions in GC and O'Donnel *ad loc.*

28 **an potius:** *or is it rather that...*; contrasting his previous hypothesis that God was in A. with the following one that he, A., is in God.

29 **etiam sīc...:** a formula following upon an anwer from scripture, namely Rom. 11:36

30 **quō tē invocō...:** *to where...* after answering one query he returns to the original, which is further complicated: if A. is *in* God, how can he call him *in*to himself?
cum... sim: causal cum clause with subj. (A&G 549)
unde veniās..: *whence might you come?* potent. subj. (A&G 443)

mē? quō enim recēdam extrā caelum et terram, ut inde in mē veniat deus meus, quī dīxit, ‘caelum et terram ego impleō’?

1.3.3 capiunt ergōne tē caelum et terra, quoniam tū implēs ea? an implēs et restat, quoniam nōn tē capiunt? et quō refundis quidquid implētō caelō et terrā restat ex tē? an nōn opus habēs ut quōquam contineāris, quī continēs omnia, quoniam quae implēs continendō implēs? nōn enim vāsa quae tē plēna sunt stabilem tē faciunt, quia etsī frangantur nōn effunderis. et cum effunderis super nōs, nōn tū iacēs sed ērigis nōs, nec tū dissipāris sed conligis nōs. sed quae implēs omnia, tē tōtō implēs omnia. an quia nōn possunt tē tōtum

---

conligō, -ere, -lēgī, -lēctus: collect, *gather* 3
contineō, -ēre, -nuī: hold together, contain 4
dissipō (1): scatter, disperse, 2
effundō, -ere, -fūdī, -fūsum: pour out, 2
ērigō, -ere, -rēxī, -rectum: raise up, lift, 1
etsī: although, even if, 2
extrā: outside; *beyond*, outside of (acc.), 1
frangō, -ere, frēgī, frāctum: break, 1
iaceō, -ēre, iacuī: lie (down), 2
inde: from there, then, afterward, 3
opus, -eris n.: work, deed, toil; *need* 2
plēnus, -a, -um: full of (abl.), 2
recēdō, -ere, -cessī: go back, withdraw, 2
refundō, -ere, -fūdī: pour back, out, away
restō, -āre, restitī: remain; *subsist*, 2
stabilis, -e: steadfast, permanent, 2
super: above, upon; beyond, more than, 3
vās, vāsis n.: vessel, 2

1 **veniās... recēdam**... 2 and 1 s. pr. act. delib. subjs., respectively (A&G 443)
quō...inde: *to what place... from that place...*
veniat: subj. in res. cl. (A&G 537) or perhaps purp. cl. (A&G 563) if we imagine that desire rather than possibility is being expressed.
3 **an implēs... capiunt:** *or do you fill (them) and it (all) subsists, (precisely) because they don't hold you?*
4 **restat... capiunt:** subj. of each is ‘terra et caelum’: A. oscillates between thinking of heaven and earth collectively and separately.
quō: *to where.*
5 **quiquid**...**restat:** *whatever remains once heaven and earth are filled*; the obj. of **refundis** is the whole clause from *quiquid* through *ex tē.*
impletō: abl. m.. sing. perf. pass. part. modifying **caelō** and **terrā**, but attracted into the gend. of **caelō** because it is nearer. (A&G 287)
opus...ut...contineаris: following certain adjs. or nouns one finds subst. noun clauses with the subj. (A&G 570-1). Translate as indicative.
quoquam: abl. of means.
6 **continendō:** abl. n. sg. of means or instrument. The abl. of the gerund rarely takes a dir. obj. in CL prose, but this rule falls away in later Latin (A&G 503a note 1; cf. G&L 427 note 3)
7 **tē plena:** abl. of means with words of filling (A&G 409a); in CL *plenus* takes the gen. more often, but in the *C.* it is reversed.
8 **etsī frangantur nōn effunderis:** *even if they are broken you are (never) poured out* 3 pl. pr. pass. subj. and 2 s. pr. pass. indic. = pr. gen. cond. (A&G 514D.1a)
et... non... nec: a rising tricolon punctuated by **nos...nos...nos...**
9 **quae... omnia: omnia** is antec. to **quae**.
jacēs (super nōs)
conligis: from *cum-lego* not *cum-ligo*
10 **tē tōtō:** abl. of means with words of filling (A&G 409a)

capere omnia, partem tuī capiunt et eandem partem simul omnia capiunt? an singulās singula et maiōrēs maiōra, minōrēs minōra capiunt? ergō est aliqua pars tua maior, aliqua minor? an ubīque tōtus es et rēs nūlla tē tōtum capit?

1.4.4 quid es ergō, deus meus? quid, rogō, nisi dominus deus? quis enim dominus praeter dominum? aut quis deus praeter deum nostrum? summe, optime, potentissime, omnipotentissime, misericordissīme et iūstissime, sēcrētissime et praesentissime, pulcherrime et fortissime, stabilis et incomprehēnsibilis, immūtābilis mūtāns omnia, numquam novus numquam vetus,

---

fortis, -e: strong, brave, valiant, 1
immūtābilis, -e: unchangeable, 2
incomprehēnsibilis, -e: unable to be grasped/understood, 1
iūstus, -a, -um: right, just, 3
misericors, -ordis: compassionate, merciful, 4
mūtō (1): change, 4
novus, -a, -um: new, 2
omnipotēns, -entis: all, -powerful, 2
optimus, -a, -um: best, noblest, finest, 2
pars, partis, f.: part; direction, side, 3
potēns, -entis: powerful, ruling over (*gen.*), 1
praesēns, praesentis: present, 1
praeter: besides, beyond (acc.), 3
pulcher, -chra, -chrum: beautiful, pretty, 1
sēcrētus, -a, -um: secret, hidden away, *distant*; *subst.* the esoteric, a secret, 4
simul: at the same time, at once, 1
singulus, -a, -um: *particular, individual*, 2
stabilis, -e: steadfast, permanent, 2
ubīque: everywhere
vetus, veteris: old, former, 2

11 **capere... capiunt:** *to hold, contain.* “Argument by rhetorical question: There are almost 700 question marks in the text of *conf.*” (O’Donnell). Twice as much as a given speech of Cicero and four times as much as a comparable sample of modern prose. It supports the notion that the *C.* was for *A.* a “liberation of questioning”—questioning which would not terminate even in paradise. (Matthews)
eandem: from *īdem, eadem, idem* “same”

12 **singula (pars)... maiōra (pars)...minōra (pars)**
singulās (partēs)... maiōrēs (partēs)... minōrēs (partēs)... *individual... greater... lesser parts (of you).*

13 **pars tua = pars tuī** in CL (A&G 143b)
ubīque tu tōtus... tē totum: *everywhere entirely... all of you.*

15 **quid...quid...:** a perhaps startling use of the neut. instead of the m. *quis* (which the use of *quis* in his third attempt highlights); it reveals how basic A.’s questions are: between the *quid* and the *quis* we can see the historical gap between the Manichaean A. of the 380’s and A. the bishop in the 390’s.

16 **rogo:** parenthetical and so does not effect the syntax of the sentence.

17 **summe (domine)... fortissime:** a string of superlatives in the vocative: “Here it is the elusiveness—the incomprehensibilty—of that reduces A. to the rhetoric of paradox” (O’Donnell).
immutabilis mutans omnia: *unchangeable (though) changing all things*. conc. part. (A&G 496).

18 **sēcrētissime**: here the root sense of *sine—cretus* “separated apart, other” is perhaps helpful in contrast to *praesentissime*, rather than the tempting derivative “secret”.

innovāns omnia et in vetustātem perdūcēns superbōs et nesciunt. semper agēns semper quiētus, conligēns et nōn egēns, portāns et implēns et prōtegēns, creāns et nūtriēns et perficiēns, quaerēns cum nihil dēsit tibi. amās nec aestuās, zēlās et sēcūrus es, paenitet tē et nōn dolēs, īrāsceris et tranquillus es, opera mūtās nec mūtās cōnsilium, recipis quod invenīs et numquam āmīsistī. numquam inops et gaudēs lucrīs, numquam avārus et ūsūrās exigis, superērogātur tibi ut dēbeās: et quis habet quicquam nōn tuum? reddis dēbita nūllī dēbēns, dōnās dēbita nihil perdēns. et quid dīximus, deus meus, vīta mea, dulcēdō mea sāncta, aut quid dicit

---

aestuō (1): be hot, *burn (w/ passion)*, seethe; have a fever, 2
āmittō, -ere, -mīsī, -missum: lose, let go, 1
avārus, -a, -um: greedy, 1
conligō, -ere, -lēgī, -lēctus: collect, *gather* 3
cōnsilium, -iī n.: plan, advice, counsel, 2
creō (1): create, 2
dēbeō, -ēre, -uī, debitum: *owe* (dat.), ought 4
dēsum, -esse, -fuī: be lacking, fail (dat.), 2
doleō, -ēre, -uī: grieve, feel pain, 4
dōnō (1): give, grant, bestow
dulcēdō, -inis f.: sweetness, 4
egēns, -entis: needy, destitute, 2
exigō, -ere, -ēgī, -actum: drive out; spend, *require* 2
gaudeō, -ēre, gāvīsus sum: rejoice (in abl.) , 3
innovō (1): renew, alter, 1
inops (inopis): without resources, helpless, 1
īrāscor, -ī, īrātus sum: become or be angry, 3
lucrum, -ī n.: gain, profit; money, 1
mūtō (1): change, 4
nūtriō, -īre, -īvī, -ītum: feed, nourish, 2
opus, -eris n.: work, deed, toil, need 2
paenitet, -ēre, -uit: it causes regret (acc.)
perdō, -ere, -didī, -ditus: lose, ruin, 2
perdūcō, -ere, -xī, -ctum: escort, guide,
perficiō, -ere, -fēcī, -fectum: accomplish, 2
portō (1): carry
prōtegō, -ere, -texī, -tectum: cover, protect
quiētus, -a, -um: quiet, calm, still
recipiō, -ere, -cēpī, -ceptum: take back 2
reddō -ere -didī -dditum: give back, return
sānctus, -a, -um: sacred, holy
sēcūrus, -a, -um: free from care, 2
semper: always, ever, forever, 4
superbus, -a, -um: arrogant, proud, 3
superērogō (1): pay over and above, 1
tranquillus, -a, -um: calm, tranquil, 1
ūsūra -ae f.: use, enjoyment, 1
vetustās, -tātis f.: antiquity, *decrepitude*, 1
zēlō (1): be jealous, love ardently, 2

21 **in vetustātem perdūcēns superbōs...** *escorting the proud into decrepitude*; ref. to Job 9:5. *per-* in composition w/ verbs often adds the meaning "all the way through/to the end, completely" and w/ adjs. "very."
et (superbī) nesciunt...: et *and yet are unaware.* see n. p. 1 for A.'s use of *et.*

23 **cum nihil dēsit tibi:** *although nothing is lacking to you*; concess. cum-clause w/ subj. (A&G 549) and dat. w/ comp. verb *desum* (A&G 370)

24 **paenitet tē:** (*lit*) *it repents you*, i.e., *you regret*; impers. verbs of feeling often take gen., inf., or *quod* of the object which causes the regret and acc. of the person feeling the regret (A&G 354)

27 **gaudēs lucrīs:** *rejoice in profit*; causal abl. with verbs of emotion (A&G 404a)

28 **supererogatur tibi ut debeas:** *it is loaned to you so that you may owe*; purp. clause with pr. subj. in prim. seq. (A&G 531.1).

30 **vīta mea, dulcēdō mea sancta**: vocatives in appos. to deus meus.

aliquis cum dē tē dīcit? et vae tacentibus dē tē, quoniam loquācēs mūtī sunt.

1.5.5 quis mihi dabit adquiēscere in tē? quis dabit mihi ut veniās in cor meum et inēbriēs illud, ut oblīvīscar mala mea et ūnum bonum meum amplectar, tē? quid mihi es? miserēre ut loquar. quid tibi sum ipse, ut amārī tē iubeās ā mē et, nisi faciam, īrāscāris mihi et minēris ingentēs miseriās? parvane ipsa est sī nōn amem tē? eī mihi! dīc mihi per miserātiōnēs tuās, domine deus meus, quid sīs mihi. dīc animae meae, 'salūs tua ego sum': sīc dīc ut audiam. ecce aurēs cordis meī ante tē, domine. aperī eās et dīc animae meae,

---

adquiēscō, -ere, -quiēvī: assent; rest, 3
amplector, -ī, amplexus sum: embrace, 1
aperiō, -īre, -uī, -ertus: open, disclose, make known, 2
inēbriō (1): make drunk, 1
ingēns (ingentis): huge, immense, vast, 1
īrāscor, -ī, īrātus sum: become or be angry w/ someone (dat.), 3
loquāx, -ācis: talkative, chatty, 1
minor, -ārī, minātus: threaten, 1
miserātiō, -ōnis f.: compassion, 3
misereor, -ērī, -itum: pity, take pity, (gen.) 3
miseria, -ae f.: misery, suffering, distress, 2
mūtus, -a, -um: dumb, mute, 1
taceō, -ēre, -uī, -itum: be silent, 3
vae: woe, 3

1 **cum**: purely temporal *cum* with indicative
vae tacentibus dē tē : *woe to the (ones who are) silent about you*; dat. m. pl. pr. act. subst. participle.
Quoniam loquācēs mūtī sunt: *because those chatty are mute*; in A.'s words, "if we cannot speak and for joy cannot be silent... what therefore shall we do, not speaking and not being silent?" A. must confess *and* confess the inadequacy of his confession, but he must also avoid the noisy chatter of the Mannichaeans who say little that is substantive. See O'Donnell *ad loc.*

3 **dabit adquiēscere... dabit ut venias... inebriēs**: *dare* + dat. and inf. means to allow someone to do something. (A&G 460.a) but *dare* can also, as here, take an ut-clause (A&G 563c)

4 **illud** = *id* in CL.
oblīvīscar: dep. 1 s. pr. dep. subj.; verbs of forgetting take the acc. when the sense is to 'completely forget' and gen. when it is 'disregard' or 'be forgetful of' (A&G 350)
ut oblīvīscar... amplectar: ; purp. clauses with pr. subjs. in prim. seq. (A&G 531.1)
amplectar: note the cluster of five dep. verbs in these three sentences.
miserēre (meī) ut loquar: *pity me so that I may speak*; purp. clause with pres. subj. in prim. seq. (A&G 531.1)

5 **quid tibi sum ipse ut... iubeās**: *of what concern am I to you, such that...* res. cl. with pr. subj. in prim. seq. (A&G 537)

6 **tibi**: ethical dat. (A&G 380)
iubeās tē amārī ā mē: *iubēre*, unlike *imperāre*, takes the acc. inf. construction (A&G 563a)
nisi faciam, īrāscāris: FLV cond.
mihi : dat. with stative, i.e., intransitive verb (A&G 367)

7 **ingentēs miseriās**: inner acc. (A&G 394)
(h)ei mihi: *woe is me! hei* is poetic in CL.
parvane (miseria) ipsa... : *isn't it misery enough if I shouldn't love you?* (Clark)

8 **quid sīs mihi**: subj. in prim. seq. in indir. quest. (A&G 330)

9 **sic dīc ut audiam**: *speak in such a way that I can hear*; res. clause with pr. subj. in prim. seq. (A&G 537)

10 **aperī**: 2 sg. pr. act. imperat.

'salūs tua ego sum.' curram post vōcem hanc et apprehendam tē. nōlī abscondere ā mē faciem tuam: moriar, nē moriar, ut eam videam.

1.5.6 angusta est domus animae meae quō veniās ad eam: dīlātētur abs tē. ruīnōsa est: refice eam. habet quae offendant oculōs tuōs: fateor et sciō. sed quis mundābit eam? aut cui alterī praeter tē clāmābō, 'ab occultīs meīs mundā mē, domine, et ab aliēnīs parce servō tuō?' crēdō, propter quod et loquor, domine: tū scīs. nōnne tibi prōlocūtus sum adversum mē dēlicta mea, deus meus, et tū dīmīsistī impietātem cordis meī? nōn iūdiciō contendō

---

abscondō, -ere, -dī: conceal, hide, 1
adversum/s: towards, *against*, (acc) 3
aliēnus, -a, -um: of another, foreign, 1
alter, -era, -erum: other (of two), 2
angustus, -a, -um: narrow, choked, 1
apprehendō, -ere, -dī: take hold of, grab, catch (TLL I.1), 1
contendō, -ere, -ī, -ntus: strive; hasten; compete, 2
currō, -ere, cucurrī: run, 2
dēlictum, -ī n.: offense, defect, sin, 2
dīlātō (1): extend, expand, spread out, 1
dīmittō, -ere, -mīsī, -missus: send (away), *forgive* 2
domus, -ī f.: house, home, 2
faciēs, -ēī f.: appearance, aspect, *face*, 1
fateor, -ērī, fassus sum: admit, 1
impietās, -ātis f. : impiety, disloyalty
iūdicium, -ī n.: decision, judgment; trial, 2
mundō (1): cleanse, clean, 2
occultus, -a, -um: concealed, hidden
offendō, -ere, -dī, -sum: offend
parcō, -ere, pepercī: spare, (dat)
praeter: besides, beyond (acc.), 3
prōloquor, -ī, prōlocūtus: because of strength of emotion call out or stumble in confessing (TLL 1.a.beta.1-2)
propter: on account of, because of (acc.), 1
reficiō, -ere, -fēcī: restore, repair, 1
ruīnōsus, -a, -um: ruinous; ruined
servus, -ī, m.: slave, 2

11 **post** *here* = **ad** in CL: *to, towards*
vocem hanc: *this saying*, referring to the previous quote '*salūs tua…*'
12 **nōlī abscondere:** *don't hide…*; **nōlī** + inf. = neg. imperat. (A&G 450)
moriar, nē moriar, ut eam videam: *let me die lest I die so that I may see it.* hort. subjs. in neg. purp. cl. and pos. purp. cl. (A&G 531.1). See expl. in Clark.
14 **angusta (nimis) est… quō veniās:** *the house of my soul is (too) choked that you should come into it…*; purp. cl. with quō is rare without the comparative in CL (A&G 531.2.a & note; cf. C&M 99b)
animae: gen. of specification (C&M 83b). A rare construction in CL.
15 **dīlātētur:** 3 sg. pr. pass. juss. subj.
habet (ea) quae offendant: rel. cl. of charac. in prim. seq. (A&G 535a).
ab occultīs meīs (delictīs)… aliēnīs (delictīs): alienus is often used as the poss. adj. of alius (A&G 113.d)
18 **et:** *even, also*; adv. use of **et** (C&M 94)
nōnne: *have I not?* expects a pos. reply.
19 **tibi prōlocūtus sum:** *I have testified (against myself) before you*; a verb pregnant with legal overtones from the Psalms (O'Donnell). Cf. *Conf*. 5.3 *Proloquor in conspectu dei mei* "I recount before the face of my God…"
20 **iūdiciō:** abl. of place where (C&M 84a)

tēcum, quī vēritās es, et ego nōlō fallere mē ipsum, nē mentiātur inīquitās mea sibi. nōn ergō iūdiciō contendō tēcum, quia, sī inīquitātēs observāverīs, domine, domine, quis sustinēbit?

1.6.7 sed tamen sine mē loquī apud misericordiam tuam, mē terram et cinerem sine tamen loquī. quoniam ecce misericordia tua est, nōn homō, inrīsor meus, cui loquor. et tū fortasse inrīdēs mē, sed conversus miserēberis meī. quid enim est quod volō dīcere, domine, nisi quia nesciō unde vēnerim hūc, in istam dīcō vītam mortālem an mortem vītālem? nesciō. et suscēpērunt mē cōnsōlātiōnēs miserātiōnum tuārum, sīcut audīvī ā parentibus

---

apud: among, in the presence of (acc.), 2
cinis, cineris m.: ash, 1
cōnsōlātio, -ōnis f.: consolation, 2
contendō, -ere, -ī, -ntus: strive; hasten; compete, 2
convertō, -ere, -ī, -rsum: turn (around), 1
fortasse: perhaps, perchance, 1
hūc: to this place, hither, 2
inīquitās, -ātis f.: injustice, iniquity, 3
inrīdeō, -ēre, -sī, -sum: laugh at, mock, 2
inrīsor, -ōris m.: mocker, derider, 1
iūdicium, -ī n.: decision, judgment; trial, 2
mentior, -īrī, mentītus sum: lie (dat.), 1
miserātiō, -ōnis f.: compassion, 3
misereor, -ērī, -itum: pity, take pity, (gen.) 3
misericordia, -ae f.: compassion, pity, 2
mors, mortis, f.: death, 3
mortālis, -e: mortal, 1
observō (1): watch, observe, attend to, 2
sīcut(i): just as as, so as, 4
sinō, -ere, sīvī, situm: allow, permit (inf.), 3
suscipiō, -ere, -cēpī: undertake, *lift (someone) up, encourage*, 1
sustineō, -ēre, -uī: hold up, sustain, 1
vēritās, -tātis f.: truth, 4
vītālis, -e: vital, pertaining to life

21 **vēritās** *may = Christus* (O'Donnell). See John 14:6.
nē mentiātur: neg. purp. cl. with pr. subj. in prim. seq. (A&G 531.1).
22 **si... observāverīs... quis sustinēbit**: FMtV w/ fut. pf. in prot. and fut. in the apod.
24 **sine me loquī**: *allow me to speak*; sinere takes an obj. infinitive (A&G 563.c)
terram et cinerem: in app. to mē.
25 **misericordia tua... cui loquor**: *it is your mercy to whom I speak*
27 **(tu) conversus miserēberis meī**: verbs of feeling often take the gen. (A&G 354)
28 **quid...nisi quia...**: *what is there... except that...*; In CL one would find an explanatory *quod* clause w/ subj. (A&G 572). This usage rarely occurs in CL.
vēnerim hūc...: perf. subj. expressing prior time in prim. sequ. in an indir. quest. (A&G 330)
hūc, in istam dīcō vitam: *to this point, in this life, I mean*; *haec*; **istam = hanc**.
29 **an**: a particle introducing the second part of a double question; often with, as here, utrum omitted in the first half. (A&G 335.a)

carnis meae, ex quō et in quā mē fōrmāstī in tempore: nōn enim ego meminī. excēpērunt ergō mē cōnsōlātiōnēs lactis hūmānī, nec māter mea vel nūtrīcēs meae sibi ūbera implēbant, sed tū mihi per eās dabās alimentum īnfantiae secundum īnstitūtiōnem tuam et dīvitiās usque ad fundum rērum dispositās. tū etiam mihi dabās nōlle amplius quam dabās, et nūtrientibus mē dare mihi velle quod eīs dabās: dare enim mihi per ōrdinātum affectum volēbant quō abundābant ex tē. nam bonum erat eīs bonum meum ex eīs, quod ex eīs nōn sed per eās erat. ex tē quippe bona omnia, deus, et ex deō meō salūs mihi ūniversa. quod animadvertī postmodum,

---

abundō (1): abound, overflow with (abl.) 2
alimentum, -ī n.: nourishment, 2
amplus, -a, -um: ample, full, spacious, 3
animadvertō, -ere, -rtī, -rsum: notice, 1
carō, carnis f.: flesh, meat, 4
cōnsōlātio, -ōnis f.: consolation, 2
dispōnō, -ere, -pōsuī, -pōsitus: arrange
dīvitiae, -ārum f.: riches, wealth, 2
excipiō, -ere, -cēpī, -ceptus: take out, 1
fōrmō (1): form, shape, 2
fundus, -ī m.: *bottom*; farm, estate, 1
hūmānus, -a, -um: human, 4
īnstitūtiō, -ōnis f.: disposition, character; *design*, 1
lāc, lactis n.: milk, 2
nūtriō, -īre, -īvī, -ītum: feed, nourish, 2
nūtrīx, nūtrīcis f.: nurse, 3
ōrdinō (1): set in order, regulate, order 2
postmodum: after a while, a little later, 1
quippe: for, no doubt, of course, 1
secundum: according to (acc.), 2
tempus, -poris n.: time, *season* 3
ūber, -is n.: udder, *breast*, 1
ūniversus, -a, -um: all together, all, entire 2
usque: (all the way) up to, continuously, 4

1 **ex quō (virō) et in quā (feminā):** i.e., from his father and in his mother (Clark).
fōrmāstī: syncopation of perf. (A&G 181).
2 **meminī:** defective verb which, like odisse, only has perfect forms but present meaning. Translate presently.
4 **īnfantiae:** personified as the dat. indir. obj. of *dare* or perhaps simply obj. gen. with **alimentum**.
5 **et (secundum tuas) dīvitiās... dispositās...:** *and according to your riches deposited...*
usque ad fundum rerum: "all the way to the humblest levels of creation" (G&M).
6 **dabās... nolle... velle:** *dare* + dat. and inf. means to allow someone to do something. (A&G 460.a)
amplius = plus in CL (Arts).
(dabas) nūtrientibus velle dare...
mē: obj. of nūtrientibus
quod: obj. of **dare**
7 **volebant dare (id) quō abundābant ex tē:** *they were willing to give that in which they abounded from you*; quō = abl. of means with verbs of filling (A&G 409a)
8 **bonum... bonum meum:** *my good from them was (a) good for them...*
10 **quod... animadvertī:** *and I noticed this...*; conn. rel. and so not a sub. cl. See next note.

clāmante tē mihi per haec ipsa quae tribuis intus et foris. nam tunc sūgere nōram et adquiēscere dēlectātiōnibus, flēre autem offēnsiōnēs carnis meae, nihil amplius.

1.6.8 post et rīdēre coepī, dormiēns prīmō, deinde vigilāns. hoc enim dē mē mihi indicātum est et crēdidī, quoniam sīc vidēmus aliōs īnfantēs: nam ista mea nōn meminī. et ecce paulātim sentiēbam ubi essem, et voluntātēs meās volēbam ostendere eīs per quōs implērentur, et nōn poteram, quia illae intus erant, foris autem illī, nec ūllō suō sēnsū valēbant introīre in animam meam. itaque iactābam membra et vōcēs, signa similia voluntātibus meīs, pauca

---

adquiēscō, -ere, -quiēvī: assent; rest, 3
amplus, -a, -um: ample, full, spacious, 3
carō, carnis f.: flesh, meat, 4
coepī, coepisse, coeptum: begin, 2
deinde then, next, 1
dēlectātiō, -ōnis f.: delight, enjoyment, 3
dormiō, -īre, -īvī: sleep, 1
foris: adv. out of doors, outside 2
iactō (1): throw, toss back and forth, 2
indicō (1): *point out*, accuse, 4
introeō, -īre, iī, -itum: go into, enter, 1
intus: within, inside, 3
itaque: and so, 4
nōscō, -ere, nōvī, nōtum: know (how), 4
offēnsiō, -ōnis f.: (cause/source of) pain, 1
ostendō (1): show, display, make clear, 2
paucī, -ae, -a: little, few, scanty, 1
paulātim: gradually, little by little, 2
rideō, -ēre, rīsī, -rīsum: smile, laugh (at), 3
similis, -e: similar to, like (dat.), 3
sūgō, ere, sūxī, sūctum: suckle, breastfeed
tribuō, -ere, -uī, tribūtum: distribute, dispose, bestow, assign, 2
ūllus, -a, -um: any, 3
valeō, -ēre, uī: be strong, fare well, be able to do (inf.) 3
vigilō (1): be awake, be vigilant, 2

11 **clāmante tē:** *because of you shouting*; m. s. abl. abs. pr. act. part. integrated into the sentence structure (A&G 419b; C&M 84c) or perhaps merely abl. abs. as subordinate clause (A&G 420)

12 **no(ve)ram: :** syncopation of perf. (A&G 181); the perf. and plupf. of *nōscō* are very often used as the pres. and impf. (A&G 205b note 2)
sūgere nōram et adquiēscere… flēre: *I knew how to suckle and to rest… to bewail…*; *nōscō* can take the inf. in the sense 'know how' (A&G 456; C&M 89b)
adquiēscere (in) dēlectātiōnibus: as opposed to **requiescat in tē** (1.1.1); abl. of place where (C&M 84a)
amplius = magis

14 **post:** *later, afterwards*; adverbial.

16 **paulātim sentiēbam:** *little by little I was becoming aware*; inceptive impf. (A&G 471c)

17 **essem:** 1 s. impf. subj., sec. seq. in indir. quest. (A&G 330)
per quōs: in CL = *a/ab + abl.* (C&M 86c)
implerentur: 3 pl. impf. pass. subj. in rel. cl. of purp. (A&G 531.2)

19 **valēbant** : often = *posse* in IL (C&M 89b)

20 **iactābam membra et vōcēs:** *I was tossing around limbs and sounds*; ex. of zeugma, where a verb "yokes" two subjs. or objs. but with two different meanings within its semantic range, one often literal and the other metaphorical.
signa: in app. to **membra et vōcēs**
similia voluntātibus meīs: we would more normally expect the gen. (*voluntatum*) in CL. (A&G 385.2)

quae poteram, quālia poteram: nōn enim erant vērē similia. et cum mihi nōn obtemperābātur, vel nōn intellēctō vel nē obesset, indignābar nōn subditīs maiōribus et līberīs nōn servientibus, et mē dē illīs flendō vindicābam. tālēs esse īnfantēs didicī quōs discere potuī, et mē tālem fuisse magis mihi ipsī indicāvērunt nescientēs quam scientēs nūtrītōrēs meī.

1.6.9 et ecce īnfantia mea ōlim mortua est et ego vīvō. tū autem, domine, quī et semper vīvis et nihil moritur in tē, quoniam ante prīmōrdia saeculōrum, et ante omne quod vel ante dīcī potest, tū es, et deus es dominusque omnium quae creāstī, et apud tē rērum

---

apud: among, at the house of, *in the presence of* (acc.), 2
creō (1): create, 2
indicō (1): *point out*, accuse, 4
indīgnor, -ārī, -ātus sum: be indignant, angry, (abl.) 2
intellegō, -ere, -lēxī, -lēctum: realize, understand, 4
līber lībera līberum: free, 3
mortuus, -a, -um: dead, 3
nūtrītor, -ōris m.: nourisher, guardian, 1
obsum, -ere, -fuī: be in the way, be against, *harm*, 1
obtemperō (1): comply with, heed, 3
ōlim: once, formerly, 1
prīmordium, -ī n.: origin, beginning, 2
quālis, -e: what sort?, 2
saeculum, -ī n.: generation, lifetime, *age* 3
semper: always, ever, forever, 4
similis, -e: similar to, like (gen. or dat.), 3
subdō, -ere, -didī, -ditum: put under, *subordinate*, subdue, 1
vindicō (1): *avenge*, punish, 2
vīvus, -a, -um: living, alive, 3

21 **pauca (signa) quae (facere) poteram**
22 **mihi obtemperābātur**: *it was being yielded to me*; impers. pass. verbs take the dat. of the pers. interested. (A&G 208d)
intellēctō (signō): *since the sign was not understood*; s. abl. abs. pf. pass. part. integrated into the sentence structure (A&G 419b; C&M 84c)
nōn obtemperābātur... nē obesset: 3 s. impf. subj. sec. seq. in neg. purp. cl.
23 **indignābar... maiōribus**: *indignārī* takes the acc. in CL and while it can be taken with the dat., "to deem oneself unworthy of" seems pointed, as our baby general barks orders and bemoans his plight.
24 **et mē dē illīs flendō vindicābam**: *vindicō* takes in IL the acc. of the person being avenged and *ab/de* + abl. of the person against whom one avenges himself.
didicī īnfantēs... esse tālēs: indir. state.
talēs... talem: *like that, i.e.,* such as A. just described.
25 **mē tālem fuisse**: indir. statement again after **indicāvērunt**, with **fuisse** showing time prior to the main verb, trans. 'had been' (A&G 584)
25 **nescientēs (infantēs)**
nescientēs... nūtrītōrēs... indicaverunt: another example of *zeugma*, where a verb "yokes" two subjs. or objs. (see prior p.)
29 **ante omne (id) quod vel 'ante' dīcī potest**: *before all that which can even be called 'before';* **ante** is the pred. nom. and **quod** the nom. Such a construction is expected with copulative verbs like *dīcere* in the pass. (A&G 283)
30 **creā(vi)stī**: sync. of perf. (A&G 181)

omnium īnstabilium stant causae, et rērum omnium mūtābilium immūtābilēs manent orīginēs, et omnium inratiōnālium et temporālium sempiternae vīvunt ratiōnēs, dīc mihi supplicī tuō, deus, et misericors miserō tuō dīc mihi, utrum alicui iam aetātī meae mortuae successerit īnfantia mea. an illa est quam ēgī intrā vīscera mātris meae? nam et dē illā mihi nōnnihil indicātum est et praegnantēs ipse vīdī fēminās. quid ante hanc etiam, dulcēdō mea, deus meus? fuīne alicubi aut aliquis? nam quis mihi dicat ista, nōn habeō; nec pater nec māter potuērunt, nec aliōrum experīmentum nec memoria mea. an inrīdēs mē ista quaerentem tēque dē hōc

---

alicubī: anywhere, somewhere, 1
causa, -ae f.: reason, 2
dulcēdō, -inis f.: sweetness, 4
experīmentum, -ī n.: test, experiment
fēmina, -ae f.: woman, wife
immūtābilis, -e: immutable, 2
indicō (1): point out, accuse, 4
inratiōnālis, -e: without reason, irrational, 1
inrīdeō, -ēre, -sī, -sum: laugh at, mock, 2
īnstabilis, -e: unsteady, unstable, 1
intrā: prep. within (acc.)
maneō, -ēre, mansī, --: stay, wait, 1
memoria, -ae f.: memory, 4
misericors, -ordis: compassionate, merciful, 4
mortuus, -a, -um: dead, 3
mūtābilis, -e: changeable, mutable, 1
nōnnihil: some, not-none, 1
orīgō, orīginis f.: beginning, origin, 1
praegnāns, -antis: pregnant, 1
ratio, ratiōnis, f.: calculation, account; reason; *principle*, 1 2
sempiternus, -a, -um: eternal, everlasting, 2
stō (1): stand (fast), stay still, 1
succēdō, -ere, -cessī: follow (on), (dat.), 4
supplicium, -iī n.: punishment, 2
temporālis, -e: time-bound, transitory, 1
utrum: whether (often with *an*, 'or'), 4
vīscus, vīsceris n.: entrails, viscera, *womb*

1 **stant...manent...vīvunt**: a rising tricolon
2 **manent orīginēs**: *the beginnings remain (beginnings)*; oxymoron, a favorite of A.'s
4 **misericors**: as often with a adjs. in appos. to the nom., translate as an adv. (A&G 290)
5 **utrum...succeserit**: 3 s. pf. act. subj., in prim. seq. of indir. quest. showing time prior following *dīc* 'say' (A&G 573;575)
7 **praegnantēs ipse vīdī fēminās**: A. bracketed by pregnant women—a metaphor?
8 **fuīne**: *did I exist?*
nōn habeō (aliquem) quis... dicat = *nōn est aliquis mihi qui...* ; rel. cl. of charac. in prim. seq. (A&G 535)
9 **pater nec māter... experīmentum... memoria**: all subjs. of **potuērunt**. Eng. 'could' is ambiguous, so translate "were not able"
10 **quaerentem**: *because I am seeking*; . nom. m. sg. pr. act. causal part.

Ille, Iste, Hic, Ipse, Is (A&G 296-298; C&M 68; Arts p. 52-56)

1. **In CL** ***is*** function like the personal pronouns he, she, it or as correlatives for *qui*. But their force weakened over time and they are often replaced by one of the other four demonstratives.
2. **In CL** ***iste*** was a second-person demonstrative signifying "that of yours" or, perjoratively, "that darned." Over time its original force weakened; still a stronger demonstrative, it took the place of *hic* and sometimes *ille*. *iste* = *hic* p. 9.28, above l. 8, p. 19 (3x), p. 37 (2x), p. 53.20 *etc.*; *iste* = *ille* p. 39.30, p. 44 (2x).

Continued on p. 15

quod novī laudārī ā mē iubēs et cōnfitērī mē tibi?

1.6.10 cōnfiteor tibi, domine caelī et terrae, laudem dīcēns tibi dē prīmōrdiīs et īnfantiā meā, quae nōn meminī. et dedistī ea hominī ex aliīs dē sē conicere et auctōritātibus etiam mulierculārum multa dē sē crēdere. eram enim et vīvēbam etiam tunc, et signa quibus sēnsa mea nōta aliīs facerem iam in fīne īnfantiae quaerēbam. unde hoc tāle animal nisi abs tē, domine? an quisquam sē faciendī erit artifex? aut ūlla vēna trahitur aliunde quā esse et vīvere currat in nōs, praeterquam quod tū facis nōs, domine, cui esse et vīvere nōn aliud atque aliud, quia summē esse ac summē vīvere idipsum est?

---

aliunde: from elsewhere, somewhere, 1
animal, -is n.: (living) creature, animal, 1
artifex, -icis m.: craftsman, artist, 1
auctōritās, -tātis f.: authority, clout, 3
coniciō, -ere, -iēcī, -iectum: bring together, unite, discuss, *understand*, 1
currō, -ere, cucurrī, cursum: run, 2
fīnis, -is m./f.: end, border; territory, 2
laus, laudis f.: praise, adulation, 4
muliercula, -ae f.: little woman
nōscō, -ere, nōvī, nōtum: know (how) 4
praeterquam: more than; except, besides 2
prīmordium, -ī n.: origin, beginning, 2
sēnsa, -ōrum n. pl.: thoughts, notions, 2
trahō, -ere, trāxī, tractum: draw, drag, 1
ūllus, -a, -um: any, 3
vēna, -ae f.: vein, artery; channel, pl. strength

11 **iubēs tē laudārī ā mē dē hōc quod novī et (iubēs) mē cōnfitērī tibi (id quod nesciō)**
12 **laudem dicēns**: *while speaking praise*; m. nom. m. sg. pr. act. circums. part.
13 **dedistī hominī conicere ea dē sē ex aliīs... (dedistī eī) crēdere multa dē sē**: *dare* + dat. and inf. of purp.. means to grant or allow someone to do something. (A&G 460.a)
15 **(quaerēbam) signa quibus... facerem**: 1 s. impf. act. subj., sec. seq. in indir. question following *quaerō* (A&G 573)
16 **unde... (vēnit)?**
sē faciendī... artifex: *the architect of creating himself*; generally one finds the gerundive for the gerund when it needs to take an obj., except when that object is a neuter adj. or, as here, a pronoun (A&G 502; cf. G&L 427 note 3)
in fine infantiae in CL = **in fine extremā**
17 **prūdentiōribus (quam mē)**
18 **quā (vēnā)... currat**: abl. of means w/ subj. in rel. cl. of char.; understand 'the sort of channel by which... could run' (A&G 535)
currat: sg. by attraction to the nearer subj., i.e., **vīvere**
aliunde... praeterquam: *from somewhere else... besides...*
19 **quod**: *the fact that*; **quod** technically stands in appos. to **vēna**, but slides into the neut. as a result of modifying the whole previous idea (A&G 572)
cui: dat. of ref.
esse et vīvere: subj. infs. supply requisite form of *esse*
aliud atque aliud: *one thing and another...*
20 **quia summē esse ac summē vīvere idipsum**: *since, to be in the highest way and to live in the highest way are the very same thing.*

summus enim es et nōn mūtāris, neque peragitur in tē hodiernus diēs, et tamen in tē peragitur, quia in tē sunt et ista omnia: nōn enim habērent viās trānseundī, nisi continērēs eās. et quoniam annī tuī nōn dēficiunt, annī tuī hodiernus diēs. et quam multī iam diēs nostrī et patrum nostrōrum per hodiernum tuum trānsiērunt et ex illō accēpērunt modōs et utcumque extitērunt, et trānsībunt adhūc aliī et accipient et utcumque existent. tū autem īdem ipse es et omnia crāstina atque ultrā omniaque hesterna et retrō hodiē faciēs, hodiē fēcistī. quid ad mē, sī quis nōn intellegat? gaudeat et ipse dīcēns, 'quid est hoc?' gaudeat etiam sīc, et amet nōn inveniendō

---

accipiō -ere -cēpī -ceptum: receive, accept, 4
annus, -ī m.: year, 3
contineō, -ēre, -nuī, -ntum: hold together, 4
crāstinus, -a, -um: of tomorrow
dēficiō, -ere, -fēcī, -fectum: fail, lose heart, faint 3
existō (exsistō), -ere, -stitī, -stitum: emerge, appear, be visible; *come into being*, 1
ex(s)tō, -āre, -(s)titī, -(s)titum: stand out, arise, exist, 1
gaudeō, -ēre, gāvīsus sum: enjoy, rejoice, 3
hesternus, -a, -um: of yesterday, 1
hodiē: today, 2
hodiernus, -a, -um: of today, today's, 3
intellegō, -ere, -lēxī, -lēctum: realize, understand, 4
mūtō (1): change, 4
neque: and not; neither…nor, 2
peragō, -ere, perēgī, peractum: carry through, pass, complete, 1
retrō: backwards, 1
ultrā: beyond, further, thereafter, 1
utcumque: in whatever manner or way, 2

22 **ista = haec**
23 **habērent… continērēs**: *would have… were holding*; pr. CTF cond. (A&G 517)
trānseundī: n. s. gen. gerund of purp.; the bare gen. gerund for purpose is rare in CL though it occurs with some frequency in Sallust (one of the central authors of late antique education), whose influence may be felt here. The gen. for purpose becomes increasingly common in IL.
24 **quam multī**: *how(ever) many*; adv. *quam*
25 **et (quam multī diēs) patrum…**
26 **ex illō (tuō hodiernō)**: that is, from God's eternal "now."
et quam… existent: no matter the number or manner of all days that all or were, they existed (or will exist) by virtue of God's "today" and end by being passed within it.
29 **quid ad mē (pertineat)… intellegat**:: *what (would it matter) to me, if… should understand*; **intellegat** is pr. act. subj. in prot. of FLV cond.
gaudeat… gaudeat… amet: 3 sg. pr. act. juss. subjs.

…Demonstratives Continued from p. 13 (A&G 296-298; C&M 68; Arts p. 52-56)

3. **In CL *ille*** meant "that distant/famous/former" and was used in contrast to *hic*, but in later Latin it can be used twice in contrast with itself (*illae… illī* p. 11.18) or as *is, ea, id* (p. 7.4), and at times nearly = *the.*
4. **In CL *ipse*** meant "self" and was often used with other (pro)nouns for extra emphasis. Like the other demonstratives, its force lessened and it at times merely = a pronoun (cf. p. 7.7, 15.29, 51.30 53.16)

Caveat lector: these lines of demarcation are often blurry and the traditional senses often kept. The reader must carefully evaluate each use according to the context. Yet it is probably good practice--with the possible exception of *ista* = *haec*--to "try on" the traditional meanings before the later ones.

invenīre potius quam inveniendō nōn invenīre tē.

1.7.11 exaudī, deus. vae peccātīs hominum! et homō dīcit haec, et miserēris eius, quoniam tū fēcistī eum et peccātum nōn fēcistī in eō. quis mē commemorat peccātum īnfantiae meae, quoniam nēmō mundus ā peccātō cōram tē, nec īnfāns cuius est ūnīus diēī vīta super terram? quis mē commemorat? an quīlibet tantillus nunc parvulus, in quō videō quod nōn meminī dē mē? quid ergō tunc peccābam? an quia ūberibus inhiābam plōrāns? nam sī nunc faciam, nōn quidem ūberibus sed ēscae congruentī annīs meīs ita inhiāns, dērīdēbor atque reprehendar iūstissimē. tunc ergō

---

annus, -ī m.: year, 3
commemorō (1): recall, recollect, cause someone (acc.) to remember (acc.), 2
congruēns, -entis: agreeing, *fitting for* (dat.) 2
cōram: face-to-face, before (+ abl),
dērīdeō, -ēre, -rīsī, -rīsus: laugh at; mock, 1
ēsca, -ae f.: food, 1
exaudiō, -īre, -īvī, -ītum: hear plainly, really hear, hear out; hear with compassion 4
inhiō (1): gape at 2
iūstus, -a, -um: right, just, 3
misereor, -ērī, -itum: pity, take pity, (gen.) 3
mundus, -a, -um: neat, elegant; clean, pure, 1
nēmō, nūllīus, nēminī, -em, nūllō: no one, 2
parvulus, ī: subst. *a child,* 3
plōrō (1): cry, wail, 2
quidem: indeed, in fact, assuredly, certainly, 3
quīlibet, quae- quod-: whoever or whatever you please; anyone, anything, 2
super: above, upon; beyond, more than, 3
tantillus, -a, -um: so little, so small, 2
ūber, -is n.: udder, *breast,* 3
vae: woe, 3

1 **nōn inveniendō invenīre potius quam inveniendō nōn invenīre tē:** 'We are speaking about God. What is strange if you do not understand? If you in fact understand, it is not God.' A. *Serm.* cxvii.5

2 **exaudī (mē):** *hear (me) out.*

4 **quis... commemorat:** *who (can) tell?*; Latin often uses the indic. to express possibility and power when English would use the subj. (A&G 437.a)
mē commemorat peccātum: commemorāre takes two acc.'s in A. instead of the CL inf. or *dē* + abl. (G&M)

5 **nec īnfāns (mundus) cuius est ūnīus diēī vīta:** *not even the infant is pure whose life is but one day old...*; **ūnīus diēī**: gen. of quality (A&G 345 note) "In general the genitive [of quality] is used rather of *essential*, the Ablative of *special* or *incidental* characteristics" (ibid.)

6 **quis...:** see n. at line 4
super terram: *super* in the sense of "upon" without implied motion takes the abl. in CL

7 **quid... peccābam:** *what was my sin?*; quid = internal acc., i.e., 'what sin did I sin'? to which *quia* gives the answer.
in quō videō... nōn meminī: *in whom I (can) see... (can) not remember*; n. line 4.

8 **an quia:** *or was it the fact that...* ; *quia* = *quod*, 'the fact that', as often in IL, answering the question from the previous line, '**quid**...' (A&G 572)
ūberibus: dat. with comp. verb.
plōrāns m. s. nom. pr. act. circums. part.

10 **sī faciam...dērīdēbor... reprehendar:** 1 s. pr. act. subj. or fut. indic. and fut. act. indic. in a fut. cond. (A&G 516b note). Emphasis is in any case on the certain fact that he would be mocked and *most justly* scolded.

reprehendenda faciēbam, sed quia reprehendentem intellegere nōn poteram, nec mōs reprehendī mē nec ratiō sinēbat: nam extirpāmus et ēicimus ista crēscentēs. nec vīdī quemquam scientem, cum aliquid pūrgat, bona prōicere. an prō tempore etiam illa bona erant, flendō petere etiam quod noxiē darētur, indignārī ācriter nōn subiectīs hominibus līberīs et maiōribus hīsque, ā quibus genitus est, multīsque praetereā prūdentiōribus nōn ad nūtum voluntātis obtemperantibus feriendō nocēre nītī quantum potest, quia nōn oboedītur imperiīs quibus perniciōsē oboedīrētur? ita inbēcillitās membrōrum īnfantīlium innocēns est, nōn animus īnfantium. Vīdī

ācriter: bitterly, fiercely, 1
crēscō, -ere, crēvī, crētum: grow (up), 1
ēiciō, -ere, ēiēcī, ēiectum: cast or throw out, 1
extirpō (exstirpō) (1): eradicate, 1
feriō, -īre: *strike*, smite; kill, slay, 1
gignō, -ere, -uī, genitus: bring forth, birth
imperium, -ī n.: command, power; *demand*, 1 (TLL 1.A)
inbēcillitās, -ātis f.: feebleness, weakness, 1
indīgnor, -ārī, -ātus sum: be indignant, angry, 2
īnfantilis, -e: of infants, 2
innocēns, innocentis: harmless, blameless, 2
intellegō, -ere, -lēxī, -lēctum: realize, understand, 4
līber lībera līberum: free, 3
mōs, mōris m.: custom, *way*; character, 3
nītor, nītī, nīsus sum: struggle, strive (inf.), 1
noceō, -ēre, -uī, nocitus: harm (dat.), 1
noxius, -a, -um: guilty, hurtful, 1
nūtus, -ūs m.: a nod, wish; beck and call 3
oboediō, -īre: be obedient, submit to, 2
obtemperō (1): comply with, heed, 3
perniciōsus, -a, -um: destructive, ruinous, 2
petō, -ere, -īvī, -ītum: seek, head for, *ask*, 3
praetereā: besides, moreover, 1
prōiciō, -icere, -iēcī, -iectum: throw forth, throw out (as trash), 2
prūdēns, -entis: prudent, sensible, wise, 1
purgō (1): cleanse, make clean, *prune*, 1
quantus, -a, -um: how much, how great, 4
ratio, ratiōnis, f.: calculation, account; *reason*; principle 2
sinō, -ere, sīvī, situm: allow, permit (inf.), 3
subiciō, -ere, -iēcī, -iectum: subject, 1
tempus, -poris n.: time, *season* 3

11 **reprehendenda**: textbook gerundive

12 **mōs reprehendī mē**: generally one finds the gerundive for the gerund when it needs to take an obj., except when that object is a neuter adj. or, as here, a personal pronoun (A&G 502; cf. G&L 427 note 3)

13 **nec vīdī quemquam scientem... bona prōicere**: *nor have I seen anyone (to) toss out the good (things) knowingly*; adjs. modifynig subj. or obj. can be translated as advs. (A&G 290)

14 **bona erant... petere...indignārī...nītī...**: subj. infs. in appos. to **bona.**

15 **indignārī... hominibus... maiōribus... hīsque... prūdentiōribus** : **indignārī** *dignus* and its cognates can take the abl. of resp. (A&G 418b), though this verb often takes the dat. in IL (TLL). But compare A.'s innovative use of *delectō* (p. 45), *inimicō* (p. 49), and *fārī* (p. 20), and his use of *meticulōsus* (p. 40).
quod... darētur: 3. s. impf. pass. subj. in rel. cl. of charac. in sec. seq. (A&G 535).

17 **multīsque... prūdentiōribus... obtemperantibus... nocēre**: dats. with stative, i.e., intransitive verb (A&G 367)

18 **nocēre**: compl. inf. with **nītī** (A&G 456)

19 **oboedītur imperiīs quibus oboedīrētur**: impers. passives of intransitive verbs take the dat. (A&G 208d; 372)

ego et expertus sum zēlantem parvulum: nōndum loquēbātur et intuēbātur pallidus amārō aspectū conlactāneum suum. quis hoc ignōrat? expiāre sē dīcunt ista mātrēs atque nūtrīcēs nesciō quibus remediīs. nisi vērō et ista innocentia est, in fonte lactis ūbertim mānante atque abundante opis egentissimum et illō adhūc ūnō alimentō vītam dūcentem cōnsortem nōn patī. sed blandē tolerantur haec, nōn quia nūlla vel parva, sed quia aetātis accessū peritūra sunt. quod licet probēs, cum ferrī aequō animō eadem ipsa nōn possunt quandō in aliquō annōsiōre dēprehenduntur.

1.7.12 tū itaque, domine deus meus, quī dedistī vītam īnfantī et

---

abundō (1): abound, overflow with (abl.) 2
accessus, -ūs m.: approach, succession, 1
aequus, -a, -um: equal, level, fair, 1
alimentum, -ī n.: nourishment, 2
amārus, -a, -um: bitter; harsh, 2
annōsus, -a, -um: aged, old, 1
aspectus, -ūs m.: sight, 1
blandus, -a, -um: flattering, pleasant, 1
conlactāneus, -ī m.: brother, one nourished at the same breast, 1
cōnsors, -consortis: companion, 1
dēprehendō, -ere, -dī, -ēnsus: seize, catch, 3
dūcō, -ere, dūxī, ductum: lead, draw, 1
egēns, -entis: needy, destitute, 2
experior, -īrī, expertus: experience, 2
expiō (1): expiate, 2
ferō, ferre, tulī, lātus: carry, bear, *endure*, 3
fons, fontis m.: origin, fount, source, 1
ignōrō (1): not know; be ignorant, 2
innocentia, -ae f.: innocence, 2
intueor, -ērī, intuitus: look at, glare at; give the evil eye 2
Itaque: and so, 4
lāc, lactis n.: milk, 2
licet, -ēre, -uit: is allowed, permitted, 2
mānō (1): drip, flow, 1
nūtrīx, nūtrīcis f.: nurse, 3
ops, opis f.: resources, *nutrition*, 1
pallidus, -a, -um: pale
parvulus, ī: subst. *a child*, 3
patior, -ī, passus: suffer, endure; allow, 4
pereō, -īre, -iī, peritum: perish, 1
probō (1): approve, commend, show, *prove* 2
quandō: when, since, 3
remedium, iī n.: remedy, cure, 1
tolerō (1): endure, sustain, bear, allow, 1
ūbertim: richly, amply, fully, 1
zēlō (1): be jealous, love ardently, 2

22 **amārō (cum) aspectū**: abl. of manner can omit *cum* in the presence of an adj. (A&G 412)
24 **mātrēs (et nūtrīcēs) dīcunt sē expiāre ista...**
ūbertim: a word-play on the literal sense of the root (*ūber*) and the metaphorical sense (*figura etymologica*)
innocentia est... nōn patī : subj. inf.
fonte lactis : gen. of description is an IL and late Latin construction (C&M 83)
25 **fonte... mānante... abundante...**
illō adhūc ūnō alimentō : *from his—at that time—only nourishment*; here abl. of source without a prep. perhaps by analogy to that of birth or origin (A&G 403.2a).
illō nearly = *eius*
26 **cōnsortem dūcentem egentissimum...**
27 **peritūra sunt:** n. pl. fut. act. periphrastic, here without the sense of intention.
28 **quod:** *and this*; connective relative
licet probēs: *it is permitted that you prove*, i.e., *you may prove*; (A&G 565 note 2)
cum = quod: *since or seeing that...*; a special use of the cum temporal clause which developed into an explanatory clause (A&G 549a)

corpus, quod ita, ut vidēmus, īnstrūxistī sēnsibus, compēgistī membrīs, figūrā decorāstī prōque eius ūniversitāte atque incolumitāte omnēs cōnātūs animantīs īnsinuāstī, iubēs mē laudāre tē in istīs et cōnfitērī tibi et psallere nōminī tuō, altissime, quia deus es omnipotēns et bonus, etiamsī sōla ista fēcissēs, quae nēmō alius potest facere nisi tū, ūne, ā quō est omnis modus, fōrmōsissime, quī fōrmās omnia et lēge tuā ōrdinās omnia. hanc ergō aetātem, domine, quam mē vīxisse nōn meminī, dē quā aliīs crēdidī et quam mē ēgisse ex aliīs īnfantibus coniēcī, quamquam ista multum fīda coniectūra sit, piget mē adnumerāre huic vītae

---

adnumerō (1): add in, *include*,
altus, -a, -um: high, lofty, tall, 2
animō (1): enliven, animate, 2
compingō, -ere, -pēgī, -pāctus: assemble, 1
coniectūra, -ae: supposition, conjecture, 1
cōnātus, -ūs: attempt; striving, effort, 1
corpus, corporis, n.: body, 4
decorō (1): adorn, distinguish, 1
etiamsī: even if, 3
fīdus, -a, -um: faithful, loyal, 1
figūra, -ae f.: form, shape, 1
fōrmō (1): to shape, form, 1
fōrmōsus, -a, -um: beautiful, 1
incolumitās, -ātis f.: security, safety, *wholeness*, 2
īnsinuō (1): introduce, *implant*, 1
īnstruō, -ere, -strūxī: equip, 2
iūs, iūris n.: justice, law, right, 1
nēmō, nūllīus, nēminī, -em, nūllō: no one, 2
nōmen, nōminis, n.: name, 2
omnipotēns, -entis: all-powerful, 2
ōrdinō (1): set in order, regulate, order 2
piget: it disgusts (acc.) to do (inf.), 1
psallō, -ere, -ī, -tum: sing a Psalm of David, 1
quamquam: although, 1
sōlus, -a, -um: alone, only, lone, sole, 3
ūniversitās, -ātis f.: the whole, entirety, 2

1 **ut videmus**: parenthetical *ut* clause w/ ind.
sēnsibus...membrīs, figūrā: abls. of means
2 **decorā(vi)stī... īnsinuāstī**: sync. of perf.
eius (corporis)
3 **(quod) omnēs cōnātūs animantīs īnsinuāstī**: *you inserted all the ensouled impusles into the body.*
jubēs mē laudāre tē: the main verb in an ocean of subordinate clauses carrying out the command (to praise God). Accordingly, *laudō* is no longer pass. as on pg. 14 ln. 11.
4 **istīs... ista... ista** = *hīs... haec... haec.*
5 **sōla ista**: the body and its entourage.
fēcissēs: 2 s. plpf. act. subj. in prot. of a mixed CTF cond.; the implied apod. is *etiam sīc sīs bonus*. (A&G 517a)
8 **nōn meminī mē vīxisse hanc (aetatem)... coniēcī quam mē ēgisse hanc (aetatem)**: acc. + inf. construction, where the pf. inf. shows time prior to the main verb.
9 **quam mē ēgisse**: **quam** could here be the same as the previous quam (=aetatem) but to avoid tautology and match the sense to what he has just discussed, the adv. *quam* makes better sense: *how it was that I acted.*
quamquam... sit: in IL *quamquam* usually takes the subj. (A&G 527d-e).
10 **adnumerāre hanc aetātem piget mē**: *to include this part of life annoys me*; impers. verbs of feeling often take gen., inf., or *quod* of the object which causes the regret and acc. of the pers. feeling (A&G 354)
huic vītae: dat. with the comp. verb **adnumerāre** (A&G 370)

meae quam vīvō in hōc saeculō. quantum enim attinet ad oblīviōnis meae tenebrās, pār illī est quam vīxī in mātris uterō. quod sī et in inīquitāte conceptus sum et in peccātīs māter mea mē in uterō aluit, ubi, ōrō tē, deus meus, ubi, domine, ego, servus tuus, ubi aut quandō innocēns fuī? sed ecce omittō illud tempus: et quid mihi iam cum eō est, cuius nūlla vestīgia recōlō?

1.8.13 nōnne ab īnfantiā hūc pergēns venī in pueritiam? vel potius ipsa in mē vēnit et successit īnfantiae? nec discessit illa: quō enim abiit? et tamen iam nōn erat. nōn enim eram īnfāns quī nōn fārer, sed iam puer loquēns eram. et meminī hoc, et unde loquī

---

abeō, -īre, -i(v)ī, -itus: go away, depart, 1
alō, -ere, -uī, altus: nourish, 1
attineō, -ere, -uī: hold near, attain, pertain, 1
concipiō, -ere, -cēpī: receive, take in; conceive, *subst. of pass. part.* ideas, 2
discēdō, -ere, -cessī, -cessum: go away, depart, 1
for, fārī, fātus: speak, say, 1
hūc: this place, hither, 2
inīquitās, -ātis f.: injustice, iniquity, 3
innocēns, innocentis: harmless, blameless, 2
oblīviō, -iōnis f.: forgetfulness, oblivion, 1
omittō, -ere, -mīsī: pass over, let go by, 1
ōrō (1): plead, beg, pray, 2
pār, paris: equal, *similar*; peer, 2
pergō -ere -rēxī -rectum: proceed (on), 1
pueritia, -ae, f.: childhood, 4
quandō: when, since, 3
quantus, -a, -um: how much, how great, 4
recōlō, -ere, -uī, -cultus: cultivate again, recall, recollect, 1
saeculum, -ī n.: generation, lifetime, *age*, 3
servus, -ī, m.: slave, 2
succēdō, -ere, -cessī: follow (on), (dat.), 4
tempus, -poris n.: time, *season* 3
tenebrae, -ārum f.: darkness, the dark
uterus, -ī m.: belly, fetus; *womb* 3
vestīgium, -iī n.: track, foot-print, trace, 3
vīvus, -a, -um: living, alive, 3

11 **quantum... attinet:** : *as far as concerns the shadows...*; in CL the idiom is *quod adtinet*, which A. himself often uses.
12 **(infantia mea est) pār illī (aetatī) quam...**
13 **quod sī:** *but if*; (A&G 324d)
14 **ubi...ubi... ubi:** rising tricolon.
15 **quid mihi iam cum eō est:** *what interest is it of mine?*
19 **et tamen iam nōn erat:** *and yet it (infancy) no longer existed (in boyhood)*
20 **quī nōn fārer:** *who could not speak;* 1 s. impf. dep. subj. sec. seq. in rel. clause of char. (A&G 535). **fārer** as a form seems to be a *hapax legomenon* (the sole occurrence) for the sake of the word play. See G&M and O'Donnell.

Gerunds and Gerundives (A&G 500-507; C&M 90-91; Arts p. 113-19)

1. **In CL *the gerundive*** (verbal adjective in *-ndus, -a, um*) could be used as an adj. or pass. periphrastic to show obligation, purpose, or necessity (the latter does not, to my knowledge, occur in this book of the *C.*): as an adj. *mihi imitandī prōpōnēbantur hominēs = men to be imitated/deserving of imitation were put before me* (p. 47); as a subst. *reprehendenda faciēbam = I was doing things that needed rebuking* (p. 16).
2. **In CL *the gerund*** (verbal noun in *-ndī, -ō, -um, -ō*) was used to highlight the action of a verb as an abstract noun and is often considered in grammar books as an infinitive with case endings. Examples of the commonest in A. are the obj. gen. and abl. of manner: *faciendī artifex = the architect of creating* (obj. gen. p. 14); *persequendō...inimīcandō = by persecuting... feeling hostility* (abl. of manner p. 49).

didiceram post advertī. nōn enim docēbant mē maiōrēs hominēs, praebentēs mihi verba certō aliquō ōrdine doctrīnae sīcut paulō post litterās, sed ego ipse mente quam dedistī mihi, deus meus, cum gemitibus et vōcibus variīs et variīs membrōrum mōtibus edere vellem sēnsa cordis meī, ut voluntātī parerētur, nec valērem quae volēbam omnia nec quibus volēbam omnibus, prēnsābam memoriā. cum ipsī appellābant rem aliquam et cum secundum eam vōcem corpus ad aliquid movēbant, vidēbam et tenēbam hoc ab eīs vocārī rem illam quod sonābant cum eam vellent ostendere. hoc autem eōs velle ex mōtū corporis aperiēbātur tamquam verbīs

---

(anim)advertō, -ere, -tī, adversum: turn (the mind) to, pay attention, notice, 2
aperiō, -īre, -uī, -ertus: open, disclose, make known 2
appellō (1): call (by name), name, 3
certus, -a, -um: reliable, sure, certain 4
corpus, corporis, n.: body, 4
doceō, -ēre, -uī, -ctum: teach, tell, 4
doctrīna, -ae f.: instruction, teaching, 2
edō, edere, edidī, editum: put forth, *make known*, publish; put on (a game), 2
gemitus, -ūs m.: groaning; moan; *grunt*, (TLL I.B; II.B), 1
memoria, -ae f.: memory, 4
mēns, mentis f.: mind, intent, purpose, 3
mōtus mōtūs m.: motion, movement, 3
moveō, -ēre, mōvī, mōtum: move, 2
ōrdō, ōrdinis m.: order, arrangement, 1
ostendō (1): show, display, make clear, 2
pareo, -ēre, -uī : heed, obey
paulus, -a, -um: little, small
praebeō, -ēre, -uī, -itum: present, provide
prēnsō (1): grasp, lay hold of, 1
secundum: according to (acc.), 2
sēnsa, -ōrum n.pl.: thoughts, notions, 2
sīcut(i): just as as, so as, 4
sonō (1): sound, resound, echo, 4
tamquam: as if, just as if
teneō, -ere, tenuī, tentum: hold, keep, *maintain*, 3
valeō, -ēre, uī: be strong, fare well, be able (inf) 3
varius, -a, -um: various, 4
vocō (1): call, summon, 4

21 **didiceram**: Though more normal in IL, in CL we would expect the subj. in indir. quest. (A&G 575c).
`**(anim)advertī**: 1 s. pf. act. indic; the omission of *anim-* is a poetic and IL construction (TLL 3.a-b).

22 **praebentēs (maiōrēs hominēs).**
paulō post: *later by a little*; abl. of deg. of diff. (A&G 414)

23 **ego ipse... prēnsābam.**
mente...memoriā: abls. of means

24 **cum... edere vellem... nec (edere) valērem**: *since I desired to make known... and since I was unable to make known...*
gemitibus: cf. Rom. 8:26 in the Vulgate: *...cum gemitibus inenarrabilibus.*

25 **ut voluntātī parerētur**: *so that there might be obeying to (my) will*; impers. pass. verbs take the dat. (A&G 208d; 372)

26 **prēnsābam**: *I was trying to grasp*; conative imperfect (A&G 471c)

28 **tenēbam hoc... vocārī rem illam**: predication in acc. inf. indir. disc.

29 **quod sonābant cum eam vellent (mihi) ostendere**: *since they were making a sound whenever they were wanting to show it (to me).*
aperiēbātur eōs velle hoc: *it was being revealed that they wanted this...*; acc. and inf. in indirect discourse.

30 **ex mōtū**: *ex* used instrumentally is not found in CL, but often in IL (C&M 87e).

nātūrālibus omnium gentium, quae fīunt vultū et nūtū oculōrum cēterōrumque membrōrum āctū et sonitū vōcis indicante affectiōnem animī in petendīs, habendīs, reiciendīs fugiendīsve rēbus. ita verba in variīs sententiīs locīs suīs posita et crēbrō audīta quārum rērum signa essent paulātim conligēbam meāsque iam voluntātēs ēdomitō in eīs signīs ōre per haec ēnūntiābam. sīc cum hīs inter quōs eram voluntātum ēnūntiandārum signa commūnicāvī, et vītae hūmānae procellōsam societātem altius ingressūs sum, pendēns ex parentum auctōritāte nūtūque maiōrum hominum.

āctus, -ūs m.: drive, driving; movement, 1
affectiō, -iōnis f.: affection, feeling, desire, 1
altus, -a, -um: high, lofty, tall, 2
auctōritās, -tātis f.: authority, clout, 3
cēterī, -ae, -a: the other, remaining, 1
conligō, -ere, -lēgī, -lēctus: collect, *gather*, 3
commūnicō (1): share, impart; communicate 1
crēbrō: frequently, crowded 1
ēdomō, -āre, -uī, -itum: tame, subdue, 1
ēnūntiō (1): announce, disclose, 3
fugiō, -ere, fūgī: flee, escape, 2
gēns, gentis f.: family, clan, 1
hūmānus, -a, -um: human, 4
indicō (1): point out, accuse, 4
ingredior, -gredī, ingressum: step in, enter + acc. is IL, whereas the verb is intrans. in CL
inter: between, among (acc.), 4
locus -ī m. (pl. loca**)**: place, region, 4
nātūrālis, -e: natural, primitive, 2
nūtus, -ūs m.: a nod, wish; beck and call, 3
ōs, ōris n.: face, mouth, 2
paulātim: gradually, little by little, 2
pendō, -ēre, pependī: hang; be suspended, 2
petō, -ere, -īvī, -ītum: seek, head for, aim, 3
pōnō, -ere, posuī, positum: put, place, 1
procellōsus, -a, -um: stormy, 1
reiciō, -ere, -iēcī: cast off or back; reject, 1
sententia, -ae f.: thought, (court) sentence, 3
societās, -tātis f.: association, alliance
sonitus, -ī m.: sound, noise, clang, 2
varius, -a, -um: various, 4
ve: or (enclitic), 1

1 **quae (verba) fiunt:** *which words are made.* **vultū et nūtū oculōrum:** *by the expression and flicking of the eyes*; abls. of means.

2 **āctū... sonitū:** *by movement and sound*; abls. of means.

3 **affectiōnem... in... ēdomitō in eīs...**: these seem to be loose uses of the preposition *in*, where the first would be in CL an obj. gen. or *in* + acc. (A&G 348) and the second an abl. of respect (C&M 88b.3)
petendīs... rēbus: a gerund made gerundive with a dir. obj. in its own case. The original form would have been *petendō rēs* (A&G 503).

4 **verba... paulātim conligēbam:** *bit by bit I was beginning to bind words together*; inceptive impf. (A&G 471c)
in variīs sententiīs locīs suīs: *with different meanings in their own (respective) places.*

5 **quārum signa (verba haec) essent:** indir. quest. (A&G 330)

6 **ēdomitō... ōre:** pf. pass. part. n. s. abl. abs. Not quite obeying the maxim that iterms in the abs. should not refer to elements in the main sentence (**signīs... per haec**)

7 **voluntātum ēnūntiandārum signa:** *signs for the purpose of annoucning (my) desires*; n. s. gen. gerund(ive) of purp.; the bare gen. gerundive for purpose is rare in CL though it occurs with some frequency in Sallust, whose influence may be felt here. The gerundive gen. of purpose becomes increasingly common in IL.
For a gerundive as gerund with obj. see n. 3

1.9.14 deus, deus meus, quās ibi miseriās expertus sum et lūdificātiōnēs, quandōquidem rēctē mihi vīvere puerō id prōpōnēbātur, obtemperāre monentibus, ut in hōc saeculō flōrērem et excellerem linguōsīs artibus ad honōrem hominum et falsās dīvitiās famulantibus. inde in scholam datus sum ut discerem litterās, in quibus quid ūtilitātis esset ignōrābam miser. et tamen, sī sēgnis in discendō essem, vāpulābam. laudābātur enim hoc ā maiōribus, et multī ante nōs vītam istam agentēs praestrūxerant aerumnōsās viās, per quās trānsīre cōgēbāmur multiplicātō labōre et dolōre filiīs Adam. invenīmus autem, domine, hominēs rogantēs

---

Adam m.: Adam, 1
aerumnōsus, -a, -um: full of trouble, distressed, 1
ars, artis f.: skill, craft, art, 1
dīvitiae, -ārum f.: riches, wealth, 2
dolor, -ōris m.: grief, pain, 4
excellō, -ere, -, excelsus: excel, 2
experior, -īrī, expertus: experience, 2
famulor, -ārī, -ātus: be a servant, 1
flōreō, -ēre, -uī: bloom, flower, flourish, 1
honor, -ōris m.: honor, glory; offering, 3
ibi: there, in that place, *then*, 2
ignōrō (1): not know; be ignorant, 2
inde: from there, *then*, afterward, 3
labor, -ōris m.: hardship, task, labor, 1
linguōsus, -a, -um: talkative, chatty, 2
lūdificātiō, -ōnis f.: mockery, derision, 1
miseria, -ae f.: misery, suffering, distress, 2
moneō, -ēre, -uī, monitum: warn, *advise*, 1
multiplicō (1): multiply, 1
obtemperō (1): comply with, heed, 3
praestruō, -ere, -ūxī: prepare, lay out, pave (a way) before someone, 1
quandōquidem: since indeed, 1
rectus, -a, -um: direct, straight, 1
saeculum, -ī n.: generation, lifetime, *age* 3
schola, -ae f.: school, 3
sēgnis, -e: sluggish, inactive, lazy, slow, 1
ūtilitās, ūtilitātis f.: usefulness, profit, 2
vāpulō (1): be beaten, 4

11 **quās... lūdificātiōnēs**: exclamatory. "Who would not choose to die... if allowed to choose either to suffer death or return to infancy?" (G&M)

12 **id prōpōnēbātur rēctē vīvere ...obtemperāre:** *this was being held out as right living, namely, to heed...*; **vīvere** is the pred. nom. of the v., whereas **obtemperāre** is in app. to **id** (where we'd normally expec *hoc*—G&M). Infs. in app. to subj. are rare in CL (C&M 89a; A&G 452.2-3)
mihi... puerō: *to me as a boy*; predicative apposition.

13 **ut...flōrērem...excellerem:** 1 s. impf. act subj., sec. seq.; an *ut*-clause following verbs of will and desire (indir. comm.) takes the subj. Translate as Eng. indic. (A&G 563) in CL **famulor** would have taken the bare dat. (C&M 86a.3)

15 **ut discerem:** 1 s impf. act subj. sec. seq in purp. clause. (A&G 531.1).

16 **litterās:** usually 'literature' or an 'epistle', but here the sense of ABC's.
quid ūtilitātis: part. gens. are regular after neut. adjs. and pronouns (A&G 346.3)
esset: 3 s. impf. subj. of sum, sec. seq. in indir. quest. following **ignorabam.**
sī sēgnis in discendō essem: *if ever I was sluggish in learning*; in past gen. cond. with impf. subj. instead of the CL plpf. indic. (A&G 514.D.2b)

17 **vāpulābam:** *I was being beaten*; a verb with act. forms but pass. meanings.

19 **trānsīre**: compl. inf. of *cogō* (A&G 456)

20 **filiīs:** a dat. of disadvantage?

tē et didicimus ab eīs, sentientēs tē, ut poterāmus, esse magnum aliquem quī possēs etiam nōn appārēns sēnsibus nostrīs exaudīre nōs et subvenīre nōbīs. nam puer coepī rogāre tē, auxilium et refugium meum, et in tuam invocātiōnem rumpēbam nōdōs linguae meae et rogābam tē parvus nōn parvō affectū, nē in scholā vāpulārem. et cum mē nōn exaudiēbās, quod nōn erat ad īnsipientiam mihi, rīdēbantur ā maiōribus hominibus usque ab ipsīs parentibus, quī mihi accidere malī nihil volēbant, plāgae meae, magnum tunc et grave malum meum.

1.9.15 estne quisquam, domine, tam magnus animus, praegrandī

---

accidō, -ere, accidī: happen, befall (dat.), 1
appāreō, -ēre, -uī: appear, 1
auxilium, -ī n.: help, aid, assistance, 1
coepī, coepisse, coeptum: begin, 2
exaudiō, -īre, -īvī, -ītum: hear plainly, really hear, hear out; hear with compassion 4
gravis, -e: heavy, serious, important, 2
īnsipientia, -ae f.: foolishness, 1
invocātiō, -ōnis f.: an invoking, invocation,
lingua, ae f.: tongue, language, 4
nōdus, -ī m.: knot, 1
plāga, -ae f.: blow, 2
praegrandis, -e : very large, huge, 1
refugium, -ī n.: a refuge, 1
rideō, -ēre, rīsī, -rīsum: smile, laugh (at), 3
rumpō, -ere, rūpī, ruptus: break, 1
schola, -ae f.: school, 3
subveniō, -īre, -vēnī: come (to aid + dat.), 1
tam: so, so much, so very, such, 2
usque: (all the way) up to, continuously, 4
vāpulō (1): be beaten, 4

21 **(nos) sentientēs tē magnum esse**: *us perceiving that you were great;* when the main verb (*invēnimus*) is past time, the pr. part. and pr. inf. show contemp. action in past time.
ut poterāmus: *as we were able*; a limiting use of the correlative **ut** (A&G 323a)

22 **quī possēs**: 2 s. impf. subj. of possum, sec. seq. rel. clause of character (A&G 535a)
nōn appārēns: *even though you weren't appearing…*; nom. m. s. pr. act. concess. part.

23 **(Ego) puer**: *(I), as a boy….*

24 **in tuam invocātiōnem (=ad tē invocandum)**: **in** + acc. to express purpose is IL; in CL we would expect *ad* + acc. (C&M 88a.1)

25 **parvus nōn parvō affectū**: *(though) little, (I begged) with no little feeling*; abl. of manner can omit cum when an adj. is present. (A&G 412)
rogabam… nē… vāpulārem: *I was begging… not to be beaten*; 1 s. impf. act. subj., sec. seq. An *ut*-clause following verbs of will and desire (indir. comm.) takes the subj. Translate into Engl. inf. (A&G 563)

26 **quod nōn erat ad īnsipientiam mihi**: *which was not for foolishness to me*; in CL we would expect the double dat. here instead of *ad* + acc (C&M 86a.2). For the meaning compare: "Not for my foolishness did you not listen, but more for my wisdom… that I might understand what I was to ask of you" (G&M)
cum…. tunc: *when… at that time.*

27 **rīdēbantur… plāgae meae**

28 **malī nihil**: part. gens. are common after many nouns and pronouns, such as *pars*, *nemo*, and *nihil* (A&G 346.1)

29 **magnum (erat)...meum**: main clause

30 **quisquam… animus…**

affectū tibi cohaerēns, estne, inquam, quisquam (facit enim hoc quaedam etiam stoliditās: est ergō), quī tibi piē cohaerendō ita sit affectus granditer, ut eculeōs et ungulās atque huiuscemodī varia tormenta (prō quibus effugiendīs tibi per ūniversās terrās cum timōre magnō supplicātur) ita parvī aestimet, dīligēns eōs quī haec acerbissimē formīdant, quemadmodum parentēs nostrī rīdēbant tormenta quibus puerī ā magistrīs afflīgēbāmur? nōn enim aut minus ea metuēbāmus aut minus tē dē hīs ēvādendīs dēprecābāmur, et peccābāmus tamen minus scrībendō aut legendō aut cōgitandō dē litterīs quam exigēbātur ā nōbīs. nōn enim dēerat,

---

acerbus, -a, -um: bitter, harsh, 1
aestimō (1): estimate, value, consider, 1
afficio, ere, affēcī, affectum: to influence, 1
afflīgō -ere, -xī, -ctum: beat, crush, 1
cōgitō (1): think, calculate (mathematically), 1
cohaereō, -ēre, -haesī: cling together, 2
dēprecor, -ārī, -ātus: pray (to avert), 1
dēsum, -esse, -fuī: be lacking, fail, 2
dīligo, diligere, dilēxi, dilectum: to love, 1
eculeus (equuleus), -ī m.: young horse, here *the rack*,
effugiō, -ere, -fūgī: flee away, escape
ēvādō, -ere, ēvāsī, ēvāsum: go out, escape
exigō, -ere, -ēgī, -actum: drive out; spend, *demand*, exact 2
formīdō (1): dread, be afraid of, 1
granditer: mightily, strongly, 1
inquam, inquis, inquit: say, 2
metuō, -ere, -uī: fear, dread, 2
pius, -a, -um: dutiful, pious, 1
quemadmodum: in what manner, how, 2
quīdam, quae-, quid-: a certain, 3
rideō, -ēre, rīsī, -rīsum: smile, laugh (at), 3
stoliditās, -ātis f.: insensitivity, toughness, 1
supplicō (1): kneel (and) beseech, supplicate 1
timor, -ōris m.: fear, dread, anxiety, 1
tormentum, -ī n.: torture, 2
ungula, -ae f.: hoof, here, *metal claws*, 1
ūniversus, -a, -um: all together, all, entire 2
varius, -a, -um: various, 4

1 **praegrandī (cum) affectū:** abl. of manner can omit **cum** when accompanied by an adj. (A&G 412)
2 **facit enim hoc quaedam etiam stoliditās: est ergō:** *a certain toughness would, I supposed, have this effect; so there is someone…*; Latin sometimes uses the indic. when English uses the subj. (A&G 427a)
quī… sit affectus: rel. clause w/ non-specific antecedents (**quisquam**) take the subj. (A&G 535 n. 2)
3 **tibi cohaerēns… tibi…cohaerendō**: in CL *cohaerō* takes *cum* + abl., but the dat. in IL and beyond.
ita…ut… aestimet: 3 s. pr. act. subj., prim. seq. in res. clause (A&G 537)
4 **prō quibus effugiendīs:** gerundive functioning as a gerund in the num. and gen. of its obj. (A&G 503); **prō** to show purpose is not found in Cl. or early IL (C&M 87h).
5 **supplicātur:** *there is supplicating*; a true impers. pass. (A&G 208d)
parvī aestimet: gen. of value (A&G 417)
dīligēns: *all the while loving*; nom. m. s. pr. act. circums. part. modifying **quisquam**.
6 **quemadmodum:** this conj. is comparing the whole previous idea, a stalwart martyr who still sympathizes with others in pain, to his own parents laughing at his beatings.
7 **afflīgēbāmur:** "An unusually long, invertebrate sentence" (G&M)
8 **dē hīs ēvādendīs**: see n. 4 **prō quibus…**
9 **scrībendō legendō cōgitandō** : s. abl. gerunds of manner (A&G 412; C&M 91b)
10 **exigēbātur**: the subj. is the work which was demanded of them.

domine, memoria vel ingenium, quae nōs habēre voluistī prō illā aetāte satis, sed dēlectābat lūdere et vindicābātur in nōs ab eīs quī tālia ūtique agēbant. sed maiōrum nūgae negōtia vocantur, puerōrum autem tālia cum sint, pūniuntur ā maiōribus, et nēmō miserātur puerōs vel illōs vel utrōsque. nisi vērō approbat quisquam bonus rērum arbiter vāpulāsse mē, quia lūdēbam pilā puer et eō lūdō impediēbar quōminus celeriter discerem litterās, quibus maior dēfōrmius lūderem. aut aliud faciēbat īdem ipse ā quō vāpulābam, quī sī in aliquā quaestiunculā ā condoctōre suō victus esset, magis bīle atque invidiā torquērētur quam ego, cum in

---

approbō (1): approve of, commend, 1
arbiter, arbitrī m.: witness, *judge*, 1
bīlis, -is f.: bile, *anger*, 1
celeriter: swiftly, quickly, 1
condoctor, -ōris m.: fellow-teacher, 1
dēfōrmis, -e: ill-formed, misshapen, 1
impediō, -īre, -īvī: hinder, impede, 1
ingenium, -ī n.: intellect, talent; character, 3
invidia, -ae f.: envy, hatred, 1
lūdus, -ī m.: game, sport; school, 4
memoria, -ae f.: memory, 4
miseror, -ārī, -ātus sum: bewail, lament, 2
negōtium, iī n.: task, business, 2
nēmō, nūllīus, nēminī, -em, nūllō: no one, 2
nūgae, -ārum f.: nonsense, trifles, jokes, *games*, 2
pila, -ae f.: ball, playing-ball, 2
pūniō, -īre, -ītus : punish, correct, 1
quaestiuncula, -ae f.: a small puzzle or problem, *a tiny (and unimporant) question*, 1
quōminus: that no, from less, 2
satis: enough, sufficient, 4
torqueō, -ēre, torsī, tortum: turn, 1
uterque, utraque, utrumque: each (of two)
vāpulō (1): be beaten, 4
vincō, -ere, vīcī, victum: conquer, overcome, defeat, 2
vindicō (1): avenge, punish, 2
vocō (1): call, summon, 4

11 **(non deerat nobīs) memoria vel ingenium...nōs**: pl. **nōs** for sg. *ego*, probably with a self-deprecating sense, *little ol' me* (A&G 143a); **deerat** takes the nearest subj. for its number.
prō illā aetāte: *in keeping with that season of life.*
12 **lūdere**: subj. of *dēlectābat.*
vindicābātur: *there was vindicating*; true imp. pass. (A&G 208d)
13 **vocantur**: used as copulative (A&G 283)
14 **cum (negōtia) puerōrum autem tālia sint**: *although the business of boys is similar (to the games of adults)*; subj. in concess. cum clause (A&G 549)
15 **approbat mē vāpulāsse**: *thinks I was justly beaten*; **vāpulāsse**: pf. act. inf. with pass. meaning; shows time prior to main v.
16 **rērum**: objective gen. (A&G 348)
pilā: abl. of means
17 **eō lūdō**: abl. of means.
impediēbar quōminus celeriter discerem: 1 s. impf. act. subj. in clause of prevention, translate 'from... ___ing' (A&G 558b)
18 **quibus maior dēfōrmius lūderem**: *by means of which I would (later), as a rather malformed adult, sport around*; pot. subj. showing subseq. action in sec. seq.
19 **aliud... magis... quam ego**: *anything else...more anger than I*; **quam** answers to both **aliud** and **magis**. A. was less angry and the examples are analogous.
victus esset...torquērētur: 3 s. plpf. and impf. pass. subjs., respectively, in a mixed past CTF condition.

certāmine pilae ā conlūsōre meō superābar?

1.10.16 et tamen peccābam, domine deus, ōrdinātor et creātor rērum omnium nātūrālium, peccātōrum autem tantum ōrdinātor, domine deus meus, peccābam faciendō contrā praecepta parentum et magistrōrum illōrum. poteram enim posteā bene ūtī litterīs, quās volēbant ut discerem quōcumque animō illī meī. nōn enim meliōra ēligēns inoboediēns eram, sed amōre lūdendī, amāns in certāminibus superbās victōriās et scalpī aurēs meās falsīs fābellīs, quō prūrīrent ārdentius, eādem cūriōsitāte magis magisque per oculōs ēmicante in spectācula, lūdōs maiōrum -- quōs tamen quī

---

amor, amōris m.: love, 4
ārdēns, -entis: burning, 1
certāmen, -minis n.: contest, conflict, 2
conlūsor, -ōris m.: fellow player, 1
contrā: opposite, facing, *against* (acc.), 3
creātor, -ōris m.: creator, founder, 1
cūriōsitās, -ātis f.: curiosity, 2
ēligō, -ere, -ī, ēlēctus: pick out, choose, 2
ēmicō (1): leap, shine, *flash out*, 1
fābella, -ae f.: short story; tall tale, 2
inoboediō, īre: be disobedient, 1
lūdus, -ī m.: game, sport; school, 4
nātūrālis, -e: natural, primitive, 2
ōrdinātor, -ōris m.: regulator, arranger, 2
pila, -ae f.: ball, playing-ball, 2
posteā: afterwards, later, 2
praecipiō, -ere, -cēpī, -ceptum: order, take, 2
prūriō, -īre: itch, 1
quīcumque, quae-, quod-: who-/whatever, 1
scalpō –ere, -sī: scratch, scratch out, 1
spectāculum, -ī n.: show, spectacle, 3
superbus, -a, -um: arrogant, proud, 3
superō (1): surpass, overcome, 2
tantus, -a, -um: so great, so much, so large, 3
ūtor, ūtī, ūsus sum: use, employ (*abl.*), 3
victōria, -ae f.: victory, 2

22 **ōrdinātor et creātor:** apposition to **domine deus**
23 **rērum... peccātōrum:** objective gens. (A&G 348)
tantum: here = *only*
24 **faciendō:** *by acting*; n. abl. s. gerund of manner (A&G 412)
25 **ūtī:** compl. inf. of **poteram** (A&G 456)
litterīs: abl. w/ **ūtī**
quās = et (volebant ut discerem) hās: connective relative.
26 **volebant ut discerem:** 1 s. impf. act. subj., sec. seq. An *ut*-clause following verbs of will and desire (indir. comm.) take the subj. Translate to Eng. indic. (A&G 563)
illī: m. pl. nom. subj. of **volēbant**
nōn enim meliōra ēligēns inoboediēns eram: *not (because I was) choosing better things was I disobedient*
27 **ēligēns... amōre:** that both are causal in sense is clear from the parallelism: *because I was choosing... because of love for...*
sed (eram inoboediēns) amōre lūdendī: n. s. object. gen. gerund (A&G 348)
amāns...victōriās et (amāns) aurēs meās scalpī : *loving... victories and (loving) that my ears be scratched...*
29 **quō prūrīrent ārdentius:** *in order that they might itch the more furiously*; **quō** is used as a conjunction in purp. clauses which contain a comparative (A&G 531.2a)
eādem cūriōsitāte... ēmicante: *all the while that same lust to know was flashing out...*; m. sg. abl. abs. pres. act. part. as a sub. clause (A&G 420.2)
30 **lūdōs:** app. to **spectācula**
quōs = et hōs: conn. rel.

edunt, eā dignitāte praeditī excellunt, ut hoc paene omnēs optent parvulīs suīs, quōs tamen caedī libenter patiuntur, sī spectāculīs tālibus impediantur ab studiō quō eōs ad tālia edenda cupiunt pervenīre. vidē ista, domine, misericorditer, et līberā nōs iam invocantēs tē, līberā etiam eōs quī nōndum tē invocant, ut invocent tē et līberēs eōs.

1.11.17 audieram enim ego adhūc puer dē vītā aeternā prōmissā nōbīs per humilitātem dominī deī nostrī dēscendentis ad superbiam nostram, et signābar iam signō crucis eius, et condiēbar eius sale iam inde ab uterō mātris meae, quae multum spērāvit in tē. vīdistī,

---

aeternus, -a, -um: everlasting, eternal, 2
caedō, -ere, cecīdī, caesus: kill, cut down, to be beaten severely, 1
condiō, -īre, -īvī, -ītus: season, spice; salt, 1
crux, crucis f.: cross, 1
cupiō, -ere, -īvī, -ītum: desire, long for, 1
dēscendō, -ere, -ndī, -nsum: descend, 2
dignitās, -tātis f.: worth, worthiness, 2
edō, edere, edidī, editum: put forth, make known, publish; *put on (a game)*, 2
excellō, -ere, uī, excelsus: excel, 2
humilitās, -ātis f.: lowness, 2
impediō, -īre, -īvī, -ītum: hinder, impede
inde: from there, then, afterward, 3
libenter: gladly, willingly, 2
līberō (1): free, liberate, 3
misericors, -ordis: compassionate, merciful, 4
optō (1): wish, desire, choose, 1
paene: almost, 2
parvulus, ī: subst. *a child* 3
patior, -ī, passus: suffer, endure; allow, 4
perveniō, -īre, -vēnī, -ventum: come through, arrive, 1
praeditus, -a, -um: endowed with (abl.), 1
promittō, -ere, -mīsī: send forth, 1
sāl, salis m.: salt, 1
signō (1): seal; sign; *pass.*: receive a sign, 1
spectāculum, -ī n.: show, spectacle, 3
spērō (1): hope (for), expect, 1
studium, -ī n.: zeal, desire, pursuit, course of study 2
superbia, -ae f.: arrogance, pride, 1
uterus, -ī m.: belly, fetus; *womb* 3

1 **ut...optent**: 3 pl. pr. act. subj. prim. seq. in res. clause (A&G 537)
2 **quōs caedī libenter patiuntur**: *whom they gladly allow to be beaten.*
3 **sī... impediantur**: iterative subj. (C&M 102c)
cupiunt eōs pervenīre...: acc. and inf. in indir. disc.
ad tālia edenda: *to put on such (shows)*; to take a dir. obj. a gerund often assimilates the gen. and num. of its object. But as we've seen, A. is inconsistent (A&G 503a note 1; cf. G&L 427 note 3). Cf. p. 4 and 17.
4 **vidē... liberā... liberā**: 2 s. pr. act. imperatives.
5 **ut invocent... (ut) līberēs**: pr. subjs., prim. seq. in purp. clauses (A&G 531.1).
7 **prōmissā** = *quae promissa est*
8 **dominī dēscendentis**: the incarnation of Christ.
9 **signō**: abl. of means
eius...eius = dominī
signābar... condiēbar: impf. inds. showing iterative act. in past time. For the meaning see explanation in O'Donnel or Clark.
10 **spērāvit in tē**: IL usage from the Greek idiom, i.e., the New Testament (C&M 88.3)
iam inde: *already from...*

domine, cum adhūc puer essem et quōdam diē pressū stomachī repente aestuārem paene moritūrus, vīdistī, deus meus, quoniam cūstōs meus iam erās, quō mōtū animī et quā fidē baptismum Chrīstī tuī, deī et dominī meī, flāgitāvī ā pietāte mātris meae et mātris omnium nostrum, ecclēsiae tuae. et conturbāta māter carnis meae, quoniam et sempiternam salūtem meam cārius parturiēbat corde castō in fidē tuā, iam cūrāret festīnābunda ut sacrāmentīs salūtāribus initiārer et abluerer, tē, domine Iēsu, cōnfitēns in remissiōnem peccātōrum, nisi statim recreātus essem. dīlātā est itaque mundātiō mea, quasi necesse esset ut adhūc sordidārer sī

---

abluō, -ere, -uī, -lūtus: wash away
aestuō (1): be hot, burn (w/ passion), seethe; *have a fever*; 2
baptismum(us), -ī n.(m.): baptism, 1
carō, carnis f.: flesh, meat, 4
cārus, -a, -um: dear, precious, 1
castus, -a, -um: pure, 1
Chrīstus, -ī m.: Christ, 2
conturbō (1): throw into confusion, disturb, 2
cūrō (1): care for, attend to, manage, 1
custōs, custōdis m.: guard, doorkeeper, 1
differō, -ferre, -tulī, dīlātus: scatter; divulge; differ; *delay,* 2
ecclēsia, -ae f.: assembly, church, 1
festīnābundus, -a, -um: hastening, quick, 1
fīdēs, eī f.: faith, trust, loyalty, 3
flāgitō (1): demand, entreat, beg, 1
Iēsūs, -ū m.: Jesus (Christ), 1
initiō (1): initiate, begin, consecrate, 1
itaque: and so, 4
mōtus mōtūs m.: (com)motion, movement, 3
mundātiō, -iōnis f.: a cleansing, 1
necesse: necessary; (it is) necessary, 1
paene: almost, 2
parturiō, -īre, -īvī, -ītum : be in labor, struggle to give birth to (acc.), 2
pietās, pietātis f.: devotion, piety, 2
pressus, -ūs m.: pressure, *cramp*, pain, 1
quīdam, quae-, quid-: a certain, 3
recreō (1): make anew, renew, 1
remissio, -ōnis f.: repetition, a sending back, 1
repentē: suddenly, 1
sacrāmentum, -ī n.: sacrament, 1
salūtāris, -e: healthful, wholesome, *salvific*
sempiternus, -a, -um: eternal, everlasting, 2
sordidō (1): be dirty, foul, 1
statim: immediately, on the spot, at once, 1
stomachus -ī m.: stomach, 1

11 **cum... essem... aestuārem**: *while I was...*; circum. *cum* clauses w/ impf. subj. The latter inceptively: *I caught fever.* **quōdam diē**: abl. of time when (A&G 423)

2 **(ego) paene moritūrus**: *nearly about to die*; nom. m. s. ft. act. part. **vīdistī... quō mōtū... flāgitāvī**; Though more normal in IL, in CL we would expect the subj. in indir. quest. (A&G 575c). Perhaps A. retains the indic. for vividness: *with what... I truly begged.*

15 **mater... iam cūrāret**: *m*3 s. impf. act. ind. pot. subj.

17 **(ex) corde castō**: abl. of origin (A&G 403) **in fidē tuā**: *by faith in you*; CL lacks this sense of *in* (p. 40 C&M); obj. gens. **(tuī)** are sometimes replaced with poss. adjs.

18 **ut... initiarer... abluerer...**: **ut** obj. noun clause following a verb of caution or effort; translate into ind. (A&G 563e)

18 **in remissiōnem**: in CL we'd expect *ad* + acc. to express purpose. (C&M 39)

19 **nisi recreatus essem**: 1 s plpf. pass. subj.

20 **quasi necesse esset**: 3. s. impf. act. subj. in in a clause of comparison (A&G 524) **ut sordidārer**: *ut* subj. noun clause w/ *necesse est* (A&G 569.2)

vīverem, quia vidēlicet post lavācrum illud maior et perīculōsior in sordibus dēlictōrum reātus foret. ita iam crēdēbam et illa et omnis domus, nisi pater sōlus, quī tamen nōn ēvīcit in mē iūs māternae pietātis, quōminus in Chrīstum crēderem, sīcut ille nōndum crēdiderat. nam illa satagēbat ut tū mihi pater essēs, deus meus, potius quam ille, et in hōc adiuvābās eam, ut superāret virum, cui melior serviēbat, quia et in hōc tibi ūtique id iubentī serviēbat.

1.11.18 rogō tē, deus meus: vellem scīre, sī tū etiam vellēs, quō cōnsiliō dilātus sum nē tunc baptīzārer, utrum bonō meō mihi quasi laxāta sint lōra peccandī. an nōn laxāta sunt? unde ergō etiam nunc

---

adiuvō (1): help, assist, 1
baptīzō (1): baptize, 2
Chrīstus, -ī m.: Christ, 2
cōnsilium, -iī n.: plan, advice, counsel, 2
differō, -ferre, -tulī, dīlātus: scatter; divulge; differ; delay 3
domus, -ī f.: house, home, 2
ēvincō, -ere, -vīcī: conquer completely, 1
iūs, iūris n.: justice, law, right, 1
lavācrum, -ī n. : place or vessel for washing 1
laxō (1): spread out, 2
lōrum lōrī n.: thong, strap, 1
māternus, -a, -um: maternal, 1
perīculōsus, -a, -um: risky, dangerous, perilous, 1
pietās, pietātis f.: devotion, piety, 2
quōminus: that no, from less, 2
reātus, -ūs m.: charge, accusation; guilt, 1
satagō, -ere, satēgī, satāctum: bustle about, concern oneself with, 1
sīcut(i): just as as, so as, 4
sōlus, -a, -um: alone, only, lone, sole, 3
sordēs, -is f.: filth; dirt, baseness, 1
superō (1): surpass, overcome, 2
utrum: whether (often with *an*, 'or'), 4
vidēlicet: clearly, plainly, *apparently*, 2
vir, virī m.: man, 1

21 **adhūc... sī vīverem:** 1 s. impf. act. iterative subj.: *as long as I was alive.* (C&M 102c)
21 **quia.. foret:** *since (allegedly) there was going to be...*; from Livy on, *fore* w/ personal endings becomes synonymous with the impf. subj. of *sum.* (A&G 540)
in sordibus: *sordēs* is regularly pl.
23 **(pater) quī nōn ēvīcit iūs māternae pietātis quōminus... crēderem:** (*my father) who did not so overcome (in me) the right of materal loyalty so as to hinder me from... believing*; 1 s. impf. act. subj. in clause of prevention, translate 'from... _____ing' (A&G 558b)
24 **sīcut nōndum crēdiderat:** *inasmuch as he had not yet believed.*
25 **satagēbat... ut... essēs:** *(she) was working hard to bring it about that... you were...*; *ut* obj. noun clause following a verb of caution or effort; translate into ind. (A&G 563e)
ut superāret: 3. sg. impf. act. subj. sec. seq. purp. cl. (A&G 531)
27 **tibi... iubentī:** *to you commanding.*
cui melior serviēbat: *whom she was right to serve*; dat. with spec. verb (A&G 367)
28 **vellem... vellēs**: impf. subjs. in pr. CTF.
29 **dilātus sum nē tunc baptīzārer:** *I was kept from being then baptized*; clauses of prevention can be introduced by—as l. 23— **quōminus** or—as here—**nē**.
bonō meō mihi: double dat., though **meō** is redundant (A&G 382 and n. 1)
30 **utrum... laxāta sint:** pf. subj. in indir. quest. (A&G 330)
lōra peccandī: explanatory (appositional) gen. (C&M 83b)

dē aliīs atque aliīs sonat undique in auribus nostrīs: 'sine illum, faciat: nōndum enim baptīzātus est'? et tamen in salūte corporis nōn dīcimus: 'sine vulnerētur amplius: nōndum enim sānātus est.' quantō ergō melius et cito sānārer et id agerētur mēcum meōrum meāque dīligentiā, ut recepta salūs animae meae tūta esset tūtēlā tuā, quī dedissēs eam. melius vērō. sed quot et quantī flūctūs impendēre temptātiōnum post pueritiam vidēbantur, nōverat eōs iam illa māter et terram per eōs, unde posteā fōrmārer, quam ipsam iam effigiem committere volēbat.

1.12.19 in ipsā tamen pueritiā, dē quā mihi minus quam dē

---

amplus, -a, -um: ample, full, spacious, 3
baptīzō (1): baptize, 2
cito: quickly, at once, 1
committō, -ere, -mīsī: commit, entrust, 1
corpus, corporis, n.: body, 4
dīligentia, -ae f.: diligence, attentiveness, 1
effigiēs, -ēī f.: likeness, statue; *image*, 1
fluctus, -ūs m.: wave, flood, 1
fōrmō (1): form, shape, 2
impendō, -ere, -ndī, -nsum: pay, 1
nōscō, -ere, nōvī, nōtum: know (how), 4
posteā: afterwards, later, 2
pueritia, -ae, f.: childhood, 4
quantus, -a, -um: how much, how great, 4
quot: how many?, 1
recipiō, -ere, -cēpī, -ceptum: take back 2
sānō (1): heal, 2
sonō (1): sound, resound, echo, 4
temptātiō, -ōnis f.: trial, temptation, 3
tūtēla, -ae f.: protection, guardianship, 1
tūtus, -a, -um: safe, secure, guarded, 2
undique: from everywhere, from all sides, 2
vulnerō (1): wound, injure, 1

1 **sine illum, faciat:** *leave him alone, let him do it*; an imperative and hort. subj.; but in CL *sine illum facere* (A&G 563c)

2 **in salūte:** *in respect to*; this sense is less frequent in CL (C&M 88b.3)

3 **sine (ut) vulnerētur:** a subj. in an imaginary *ut*-clause (565 & n.) *sino* took the acc. and inf. in CL but in early and late latin takes the subj., without or without *ut.*

4 **quantō ergō melius et cito sānārer:** *by how much better—and swiftly too—therefore, might I have been healed.*
sānārer... agerētur: 1 and 3 p. impf. pass. pot. subjs.

5 **agerētur... meā dīligentiā ut... esset: ut** obj. noun clause following a verb of caution or effort. (A&G 563e).
quī dedissēs: pot. subj.; plpf. indicating prior time in sec. seq.; **quī** picks up the implied antecedent in **tuā**

6 **melius vērō (fuisset)** or **ita melius (fuit) verō**: is A. saying it would have been better the way he described or that it was better the way it actually turned out?

7 **quot et quantī... vidēbantur, nōverat...:** indir. quest. with the indic. (C&M 96)

8 **unde = ex quibus (flūctibus)**; A. is paritculary fond of using *unde, ubi*, and *inde* in place of relatives and demonstratives (O'Donnell)
(Deō) terram per eōs (flūctūs) ... (potius) quam ... effigiem committere volēbat: *she wanted to entrust the earth (to God) in them ...rather than the (new) image itself.*
effigiēs = A. post baptism. See O'Donnell or Clark for discussion of this (difficult) passage.
unde posteā fōrmārer: *in order that I might be moulded from (by) them*; rel. cl. of purp.; this instrumental use of *ex* only becomes common in IL (C&M 87e.1)

adulēscentiā metuēbātur, nōn amābam litterās et mē in eās urgērī ōderam, et urgēbar tamen et bene mihi fīēbat. nec faciēbam ego bene (nōn enim discerem nisi cōgerer; nēmō autem invītus bene facit, etiamsī bonum est quod facit), nec quī mē urgēbant bene faciēbant, sed bene mihi fīēbat abs tē, deus meus. illī enim nōn intuēbantur quō referrem quod mē discere cōgēbant, praeterquam ad satiandās īnsatiābilēs cupiditātēs cōpiōsae inopiae et ignōminiōsae glōriae. tū vērō, cui numerātī sunt capillī nostrī, errōre omnium quī mihi īnstābant ut discerem ūtēbāris ad ūtilitātem meam, meō autem, quī discere nōlēbam, ūtēbāris ad

---

adulēscentia, -ae f.: youth, 1
capillus, -ī m.: hair, 1
cōpiōsus, -a, -um: abundant, plentiful, 2
cupiditās, -tātis f.: desire, eagerness, *lust*, 3
etiamsī: even if, 3
glōria, -ae, f.: glory, fame, 1
ignōminiōsus, -a, -um : shameful, 1
inopia, -ae f.: need, poverty, 1
īnsatiābilis, -e: insatiable, 1
īnstō, -āre, -stitī: stand, press (on), put pressure on, insist; 2
intueor, -ērī, intuitus: look at, glare at; give the evil eye 2
invītus, -a, -um: unwilling, 2
metuō, -ere, -uī: fear, dread, 2
nēmō, nūllīus, nēminī, -em, nūllō: no one, 2
numerō (1): count, 2
praeterquam: more than; except, besides 2
referō, -ferre, -tulī, -lātum: report, bring back, 1
satiō (1): satisfy, sate, 1
ūtilitās, ūtilitātis f.: usefulness, profit, 2
ūtor, ūtī, ūsus sum: use, employ (*abl.*), 3

11 **mihi… metuēbātur**: dat. of agent with a pass. verb; such a loose use of the dat. of ag. was uncommon in CL but became common in the poets and IL (A&G 375a)

12 **ōderam mē urgērī**: *ōdisse*, like *memini* (and often *noscere*) use pf. system forms with pres. system meanings; the acc. and inf. construction with *ōdisse* is an IL construction (C&M 89f)
fīēbat: the pass. of facere w/ pr. forms.

13 **nōn enim discerem nisi cōgerer**: *I would not have (ever) learned unless I was being forced (every time)*; the impf. subj. in the protasis does not set up a CTF cond. but simply indicates a repeated action (A&G 518c).
nēmō… facit: the point is about motives: unless someone *wills* the good in the good thing he does, he does not do good.

16 **quō referrem**: *to what end I might put to use…*; adv. **quō** setting up indir. statement, though the deliberative element seems to me strong. The direct form would be, 'to what end might I put it (the learning) to use?' **referrem** is impf. because we are in sec. seq.

17 **ad satiandās… cupiditātēs**: gerundive functioning as a gerund in the num. and gen. of its obj. (A&G 503)
inopiae… glōriae: obj. gens. (A&G 347)

18 **cui numerātī**: dat. of agent with pf. pass. part. (A&G 375)

19 **errōre…ūtēbāris**: *utor* takes the abl.
īnstābant (mihi) ut discerem: *they were forcing me to learn*; An *ut*-clause following verbs of will and desire (indir. comm.) take the subj. Translate to Eng. indic. or inf. (A&G 563)

20 **meō (errōre)**

poenam meam, quā plectī nōn eram indignus, tantillus puer et tantus peccātor. ita dē nōn bene facientibus tū bene faciēbās mihi et dē peccante mē ipsō iūstē retribuēbās mihi. iussistī enim et sīc est, ut poena sua sibi sit omnis inōrdinātus animus.

1.13.20 quid autem erat causae cūr Graecās litterās ōderam, quibus puerulus imbuēbar? nē nunc quidem mihi satis explōrātum est. adamāveram enim latīnās, nōn quās prīmī magistrī sed quās docent quī grammaticī vocantur. nam illās prīmās, ubi legere et scrībere et numerāre discitur, nōn minus onerōsās poenālēsque habēbam quam omnēs Graecās. unde tamen et hoc nisi dē peccātō

---

adamō, -āre, -āvī, -ātum: (fall in) love, 1
causa, -ae f.: reason, 2
cūr: why, 2
doceō, -ēre, -uī, -ctum: teach, tell, 4
explōrō (1): investigate, test (by experience); explore, 1
imbuō, -uere: wet, soak; initiate, instruct, 1
indignus, -a, -um: unworthy, undeserving, 1
inōrdinātus, -a, -um: disordered, 1
iūstus, -a, -um: right, just, 3
Latīnus, -a, -um: Latin, 2
numerō (1): count, 2
onerōsus, -a, -um: burdensome, 1
peccātor, -ōris m.: sinner, 1
plectō, -ere: beat; punish, 1
poena, -ae, f.: punishment, 3
poenālis, -e: of punishment, penal, punitive, 3
puerulus, -ī m.: little boy 1
quidem: indeed, in fact, assuredly, certainly, 3
retribuō, -ere, -uī, -ūtus: give back, return; restore justice through punishment, 1
satis: enough, sufficient, 4
tantillus, -a, -um: so little, so small, 2
tantus, -a, -um: so great, so much, so large, 3
vocō (1): call, summon, 4

21 **quā:** *in virtue of which*; abl. of cause. **plectī... indignus:** *dignus* (and its cognates) + the inf. is a poetic and IL construction; in CL we would expect either the abl. or else a rel. cl. of char. (C&M 89e; A&G 418b)

22 **dē nōn bene facientibus... dē peccante mē:** *from those not doing good... from me sinning...*; **dē** as indicating the source or point of separation is hardly distinguishable for means or instrument, an IL usage (C&M 87d).

23 **ipsō:** could go with **mē** or **mihi**, but perhaps better w/ **mihi** to signal a shift in construction (to the obj. of **retribuēbās**); **mihi:** dat. with special verb (A&G 367) **sīc... ut... sit**: 3 s. pr. subj. of sum in res. cl. prim. seq, which **sīc** leads us to expect (A&G 537)

24 **iussistī... ut omnis animus sibi sit poena sua** : *so that every soul is to itself its own punishment*; *iubeō* pairs with acc./inf. in CL in contrast to *imperō* (A&G 563a). But here perhaps the intervening **sīc est** gives the addeed sense of a result clause

25 **quid... causae:** part. gen. w/ an (interogative) pronoun (A&G 346a.3) **ōderam:** pf. forms w/ pr. meanings.

26 **mihi :** dat. of agent w/ pf. pass. part. (A&G 375)

27 **adamāveram**: plpf. for pf. (C&M 78a) **latīnās... quās... quās... illās... onerōsās poenālēsque...Graecās**: supply *litterās* throughout.

28 **(iī) quī ...:** subj. of **docent** **legere... scrībere... numerāre:** inf. subjs. of **discitur**, which takes the number of the nearest subj.

30 **habēbam:** *I was considering*

et vānitāte vītae, quā cārō eram et spīritus ambulāns et nōn revertēns? nam ūtique meliōrēs, quia certiōrēs, erant prīmae illae litterae quibus fīēbat in mē et factum est et habeō illud ut et legam, sī quid scrīptum inveniō, et scrībam ipse, sī quid volō, quam illae quibus tenēre cōgēbar Aenēae nesciō cuius errōrēs, oblītus errōrum meōrum, et plōrāre Dīdōnem mortuam, quia sē occīdit ab amōre, cum intereā mē ipsum in hīs ā tē morientem, deus, vīta mea, siccīs oculīs ferrem miserrimus.

1.13.21 quid enim miserius miserō nōn miserante sē ipsum et flente Dīdōnis mortem, quae fīēbat āmandō Aenēān, nōn flente

---

ambulō (1): walk, 2
amor, amōris m.: love, 4
cārus, -a, -um: dear, precious
certus, -a, -um: certain, reliable,, sure, 4
Dīdō, Dīdōnis f.: Dido, 3
ferō, ferre, tulī, lātus: carry, bear, endure, 3
intereā: meanwhile, 1
miseror, -ārī, -ātus sum: bewail, lament, 2
mors, mortis, f.: death, 3
occīdō, -ere, occīdī, occīsum: kill
plōrō (1): cry, wail, 2
revertō, -ere, reversī: turn back, return
siccus, -a, -um: dry
spīritus, -ūs m.: spirit; breath
teneō, -ere, tenuī, tentum: hold, keep, *maintain*, 3
vānitās, -ātis f.: emptiness; fickleness, folly, *vanity*, 4

1 **(dē) vānitāte**
quā: abl. of cause if referring to *vanitas*, or perhaps generally locative if to *vita*.
3 **meliōrēs... litterae... quam illae:** comparison with **quam**
quibus fīēbat in mē; factum est; et habeō illud ut et legam: *by which it was being done in me and it has been done and I (now) have this*...three ways of saying that his learning to read and write was *truly accomplished*; the last being a subst. noun clause in appos. to **illud** (A&G 570)
et habeō illud ut et legam : *ut*-substantive noun-clause in app. to **illud** (A&G 570)
4 **sī (ali)quid... inveniō:** *if I find something written*; after *sī, nisī, num* or *nē, ali* takes a holiday.
sī quid (scrībendum esse) volō : *if I want something to be written*; (A&G 500)
5 **tenēre... plōrāre:** compl. infs. w/ **cōgēbar** (A&G 457)
errōrēs: 'the antonym to *peregrinatio* in the *C.*' (O'Donnell)
errōrum meōrum: gen. with verbs of forgetting (A&G 350)
Aenēae nesciō-cuius: 'contains a certain air of mild disdain' (O'Donnell)
6 **Dīdōnem mortuam:** *the death (dying) of Dido*; *ab urpe condita* construction (A&G 497)
sē occīdit ab amōre: abl. of cause usually takes the bare ablative, here perhaps emphasizing the aspect of separation in parallel to **ā tē morientem** (A&G 404)
7 **cum...ferrem**: *all the while I...* circumst. *cum*-cl. (A&G 546)
siccīs (cum) oculīs: abl. of manner omits *cum* when accompanied by adj. (A&G 412)
9 **miserō nōn miserante:** abl. of comparison (A&G 406)
10 **āmandō Aenēān**: abl. n. sg. gerund of means/instrument. The abl. of the gerund rarely takes a dir. obj. in CL prose, but this distinction fades in later Latin (A&G 503a note 1; cf. G&L 427 note 3).

autem mortem suam, quae fīēbat nōn āmandō tē, deus, lūmen cordis meī et pānis ōris intus animae meae et virtūs marītāns mentem meam et sinum cōgitātiōnis meae? nōn tē amābam, et fornicābar abs tē, et fornicantī sonābat undique: 'eugē! eugē!' amīcitia enim mundī huius fornicātiō est abs tē et 'eugē! eugē!' dīcitur ut pudeat, sī nōn ita homō sit. et haec nōn flēbam, et flēbam Dīdōnem extīnctam ferrōque extrēma secūtam, sequēns ipse extrēma condita tua relictō tē et terra iēns in terram. et sī prohibērer ea legere, dolērem, quia nōn legerem quod dolērem. tālī dēmentiā honestiōrēs et ūberiōrēs litterae putantur quam illae

---

amīcitia, -ae, f.: friendship, 2
cōgitātio, -tiōnis f.: thought, reflection, 2
condō, -ere, condidī, -ditum: found; store away, hide; *create*, 1
dēmentia, -ae f.: madness, folly, 1
Dīdō, Dīdōnis f.: Dido, 3
doleō, -ēre, -uī: grieve, feel pain, 4
eō, īre, iī/īvī, itum: go, 3
eugē: hurray, bravo, 4
extinguō, -ere, -trīnxī, -tinctum: put out, extinguish; kill, destroy, 1
extrēmus, -a, -um: outermost, farthest, last; end (of life), 2
ferrum, -ī n.: iron; sword, tool, 1
fornicātiō, -ōnis f.: fornication, 1
fornicor, -ārī, fornicātus: fornicate, 2
honestus, -a, -um: respectable, honorable, 2
intus: within, inside, 3
lūmen, lūminis n.: light, 1
marītō (1): give in marriage, 1
mēns, mentis f.: mind, intent, purpose, 3
mors, mortis, f.: death, 3
mundus, -ī m.: world, 1
ōs, ōris n.: face, mouth, 2
pānis, -is m.: bread, 1
prohibeō, -ēre, -uī, -itus: keep off, prohibit, 1
pudeō, -ēre, -duī: make ashamed, 1
putō (1): think, consider, 2
relinquō, -ere, -līquī, -lictum: leave behind, 1
sequor, -ī, secūtus: follow, pursue; chase; seek, 4
sinus, -ūs m.: fold, pocket, lap; curve, 1
sonō (1): sound, resound, echo, 4
ūber (ūberis): fertile, 1
undique: from everywhere, from all sides, 2
virtūs, -ūtis f.: virtue, power, valor, 2

12 **cordis… ōris** : object. and subj. gens.
animae: either poss. gen. or appositional gen. (C&M 83b)
14 **fornicantī (mihi)**
eugē! eugē: *well done!*; neither O'Donnell nor Clark appear to mention that this is the word used by the master to his *faithful* servants in the parable of the talents (Lk. 19:17). A. uses it again at 10.36.59 where God as *dominus* is palpable.
15 **mundī huius**: object. gen.
17 **flēbam Dīdōnem extīnctam (esse) ferrōque (flēbam) extrēma secūtam (esse)**: inf./acc. cstr. w/ *flēre*; the fact that *extinguō* is act. and *sequor* dep. feels awkward in translation. **Dīdōnem extīnctam** could also be explained as the *ab urpe condita* constructoin (A&G 497)
18 **extrēma condita tua**: *the furthest ends of your creation*; **condita** = subst. the meaning "creation" is not CL.
19 **prohibērer… legere**: (A&G 457, 558b n.)
sī prohibērer…dolērem:This iterative use of the subj. with **sī** is IL (C&M 102)
quia nōn legerem: since **quia** doesn't usually take the subj., understand **legerem** as pot. (A&G 540 n. 1)
quod dolērem: rel. cl. of ch. in sec. seq. (A&G 535§2)
20 **tālī dēmentiā** : abl. of cause

quibus legere et scrībere didicī.

1.13.22 sed nunc in animā meā clāmet deus meus, et vēritās tua dicat mihi, 'nōn est ita, nōn est ita.' melior est prōrsus doctrīna illa prior. nam ecce parātior sum oblīvīscī errōrēs Aenēae atque omnia eius modī quam scrībere et legere. at enim vēla pendent līminibus grammaticārum scholārum, sed nōn illa magis honōrem sēcrētī quam tegimentum errōris significant. nōn clāment adversus mē quōs iam nōn timeō, dum cōnfiteor tibi quae vult anima mea, deus meus, et adquiēscō in reprehēnsiōne malārum viārum meārum, ut dīligam bonās viās tuās, nōn clāment adversus mē venditōrēs

---

adquiēscō, -ere, -quiēvī: assent; rest, 3
adversum/s: towards, *against*, (acc) 3
at: but; mind you; but, you say, 4
dīligō, -ere, -lēxī, -lēctum: love, esteem, 2
doctrīna, -ae f.: instruction, teaching, 2
dum: while, as long as, until, 2
honor, -ōris m.: honor, glory; offering, 3
līmen, līminis n.: threshold, 2
parātus, -a, -um: prepared, 1
pendō, -ere, pependī, pensum: weigh, pay, 2
prior, prius: before, earlier (comp. prīmus), 4
prōrsus: straightway; absolutely, by far, 1
reprehēnsiō, -iōnis f.: criticism, blame, 1
schola, -ae f.: school, 3
sēcrētus, -a, -um: secret, hidden away, distant; *subst. the esoteric, a secret*, 4
significō (1): indicate, show; mean, 1
tegimentum, -ī n. : a covering, cover, 1
timeō, -ēre, -uī: fear, be afraid of, 2
vēlum, -ī n.: sail, awning, canvas; *curtain*, 1
venditor, -ōris m.: vendor, seller, 1
vēritās, -tātis f.: truth, 4

21 **quibus (literīs)**: abl. of means
legere et scrībere: compl. infs. of **didicī**
24 **parātior oblīvīscī**: like the verb and participle from which it comes, this adj. takes here the inf. of purp. (A&G 460); in CL *ad*+ gerund or gerundive would be more normal.
oblīvīscī: dep. pr. "act." inf. (A&G 350)
25 **at enim...sed**: *to be sure...but nevertheless*; "[*at enim*] introduces...a possible objection to A.'s position, and is followed...by A.'s rejoinder...marked by an adversative conjunction" (O'Donnell)
liminibus: loc. abl. (C&M 84a)
27 **(eī) nōn clāment... clāment** : juss. subjs. (A&G 439a). **nōn** for **nē** in prohibitions is post-classical (C&M 75.e)
28 **quōs (venditores grammaticae)**
iam nōn timeō : *...I no longer fear*
29 **adquiēscō in reprehēnsiōne** : A. oscillates with this construction between *in* + abl. and the bare abl (cf. p. 7 and 11)
30 **ut dīligam**: 1 sg. pr. act. subj. in purp. cl.
nōn clāment :asyndeton ; juss. subj.

The Gerund-Gerundive Swap (A&G 500-507; C&M 90-91; Arts p. 113-19)

1. **In CL *the gerund***, when it needed to take an object, took on the gender and number of its object while retaining its case. The CL construction is common in A.: *rēbus persuādendīs sententiīsque explicandīs = for arguing cases and explaining (court) opinions* (p. 43); *ad satiandās... cupiditātēs = for satisfying lusts*; compare the "original" forms *rēs persuādendō* and *ad satiandum cupiditātēs* (p. 32).
2. **But in later Latin** this distinction was not always made and gerunds often took objects--most often neut. pls.: *dīvīna tribuendō = by assigning divine things*...(p. 42); but A. extends this even to normal nouns: *cōnfitendō miserātiōnēs tuās = in confessing your mercies* (p. 40).

grammaticae vel ēmptōrēs, quia, sī prōpōnam eīs interrogāns, utrum vērum sit quod Aenēān aliquandō Carthāginem vēnisse poēta dīcit, indoctiōrēs nescīre sē respondēbunt, doctiōrēs autem etiam negābunt vērum esse. at sī quaeram quibus litterīs scrībātur Aenēae nōmen, omnēs mihi quī haec didicērunt vērum respondent secundum id pactum et placitum quō inter sē hominēs ista signa firmārunt. item sī quaeram quid hōrum maiōre vītae huius incommodō quisque oblīvīscātur, legere et scrībere an poētica illa figmenta, quis nōn videat quid respōnsūrus sit, quī nōn est penitus oblītus suī? peccābam ergō puer cum illa inānia istīs ūtiliōribus

---

aliquandō: sometimes, at some time, 2
at: but; mind you; but, you say, 4
Carthāgō, -inis f.: Carthage, 1
doctus, -a, -um: learned, taught, 1
ēmptor, -ōris m.: buyer, 1
figmentum, -ī n.: picture, image; creation; figment, act of (vain) imagination, 2
firmō (1): strengthen, support, 1
inānis, is: empty; vain, groundless; *subst.*: trivialities, 2
incommodus, -a, -um: inconvenient, unsuitable; *subst.* a loss, disadvangtage, 1
indoctus, -a, -um: untaught, ignorant, 1
inter: between, among (acc.), 4
interrogō (1): ask, inquire, 1
item: also, likewise, in like manner, 1
negō (1): deny, say that…not, 1
nōmen, nōminis, n.: name, 2
pactum, -ī n.: pact, agreement, 4
penitus: within, inwardly; deeply, utterly, 1
placeō, -ēre, -uī, placitum: please, be pleasing, pf. part. subst.: something agreed upon, prescription, principle, 3
poēta, -ae m.: poet, 2
poēticus, -a, -um: relating to (a) poet(ry), 2
quisque, quidque: each one or person, 1
respondeō, -ēre, -dī, -ōnsus: answer, 3
secundus, -a, -um: following, favorable, 3
ūtilis, -e: useful, 3
utrum: whether (often with *an*, 'or'), 4

1 **sī prōpōnam… respondēbunt… negabunt… ; sī quaeram… respondent…** modified FLV conditions (A&G 516.2b)

2 **utrum… sit… quibus litterīs scrībātur:** indir. quests. with subj. (A&G 330-331) **quod… dīcit**: 'fact that' **quod**-clause (A&G 572) as subject of the verb **sit.** **Carthāginem**: acc. of place to which with names of cities, towns, and small islands (A&G 427.2) **Aenēān vēnisse dīcit**: acc. and inf. indirect statement, where **vēnisse** indicates prior-time in primary sequence

7 **firmārunt**: syncopation of pf. (A&G 181) **sī quaeram…quid respōnsurus sit:** FLV cond. again but now because of the indir. quest. (and the lack of a fut. subj. in Latin) A. uses the fut. periphrastic in the subj. (A&G 575a) **quid… oblīvīscātur…**: indir. quest. (A&G 330-331) When the obj. is n. verbs of forgetting often take the acc. without difference of meaning (A&G 350b n. 1); **quid horum** = *uter* in CL (C&M 69a) **(cum) maiōre… incommodō:** abl. of manner can drop **cum** if modified by an adj.

8 **legere et scrībere:** direct objects in app. to the **quid** of the previous line.

9 **quis nōn videat**: apod. of pr. CTF **penitus oblītus suī**: The felt need for **penitus** to strenghten the verb seems to reinforce the idea that *obliviscor* + gen. means be "careless of".

10 **istīs** = *hīs*

amōre praepōnēbam, vel potius ista ōderam, illa amābam. iam vērō ūnum et ūnum duo, duo et duo quattuor, odiōsa cantiō mihi erat, et dulcissimum spectāculum vānitātis, equus ligneus plēnus armātīs et Troiae incendium atque ipsīus umbra Creūsae.

1.14.23 cūr ergō Graecam etiam grammaticam ōderam tālia cantantem? nam et Homērus perītus texere tālēs fābellās et dulcissimē vānus est, mihi tamen amārus erat puerō. crēdō etiam Graecīs puerīs Vergilius ita sit, cum eum sīc discere cōguntur ut ego illum. vidēlicet difficultās, difficultās omnīnō ēdiscendae linguae peregrīnae, quasi felle aspergēbat omnēs suāvitātēs

---

amārus, -a, -um: bitter; harsh, 2
amor, amōris m.: love, 4
armō (1): equip, arm, 1
aspergō, -ere, -sī, -sus: sprinkle upon, 1
cantō (1): sing, 1
cantiō, -iōnis f.: song, incantation, 1
Creūsa, -ae f.: Creusa, 1
cūr: why, 2
difficultās, -tātis f.: trouble, difficulty, 2
dulcis, -e: sweet, pleasant, 4
duo, duae, duo: two, 4
ēdiscō, -ere, -didicī: learn thoroughly, 1
equus, -ī m.: horse, 2
fābella, -ae f.: short story, tall tale, 2
fel, fellis n.: the gall bladder; gall
Homērus, ī m.: Homer, 2
incendium, -iī n.: fire, conflagration, 1
ligneus, -a, -um: wooden, 1
lingua, ae f.: tongue, language, 4
odiōsus, -a, -um: hateful, odious, 1
omnīnō: altogether, (strengthens neg.) *at all* 4
peregrīnus, -ī m.: stranger, foreigner, 1
perītus, -a, -um: skilled, experienced, *clever* 1
plēnus, -a, -um: full, 2
praepōnō, -ere, -posuī: put in charge over; place before, prefer, 1
quattuor: four, 1
spectāculum, -ī n.: show, spectacle, 3
suāvitās, -ātis f.: sweetness, 1
texō, -ere, -uī, textum: weave, 1
Troia, -ae f.: Troy, 1
umbra, -ae f.: shade, shadow, 1
vānitās, -ātis f.: emptiness; fickleness, folly, 4
Vergilius, -iī m.: Vergil, 1
vidēlicet: clearly, plainly, 2

11 **amōre**: abl. of respect (A&G 418)
ista= haec
13 **spectāculum vānitātis = spectāculum vanum** ; appositional genitive (C&M 83b)
equus… Creūsae : in apposition to **spectāculum**
plēnus armātīs: abl. of means with words of filling (A&G 409a)
15 **oderam**: *odisse* has pf. system forms with pr. system meanings (A&G 476)
16 **perītus texere**: epexegetical or Greek inf. (A&G 461)
17 **crēdō… ita sit**: *For Greek boys, I suppose, Vergil would be similar.* Take **crēdō** as parenthetical and **sit** as pot. subj. or as an apod. of an implied *sī*-clause in **cum… coguntur** (A&G 542). As in the case of most parenthicals, one would expect **crēdō** to be somewhere other than first position (A&G 599c), but for this verb first-position is normal (L&S II.B.2b(γ)).
mihi… puero : *to me… as a boy anyway.*
18 **sīc… ut**: correllative (A&G 323)
19 **illum**: in sense of 'that famous' (A&G 297b)
20 **quasi (difficultas) aspergēbat**: normally we'd expect the **subj.** with **quasi** but here A. is stating a fact (A&G 524)

Graecās fābulōsārum nārrātiōnum. nūlla enim verba illa nōveram, et saevīs terrōribus ac poenīs ut nōssem īnstābātur mihi vehementer. nam et latīna aliquandō īnfāns ūtique nūlla nōveram, et tamen advertendō didicī sine ūllō metū atque cruciātū, inter etiam blandīmenta nūtrīcum et ioca adrīdentium et laetitiās adlūdentium. didicī vērō illa sine poenālī onere urgentium, cum mē urgēret cor meum ad parienda concepta sua, quae nōn possem, nisi aliqua verba didicissem nōn ā docentibus sed ā loquentibus, in quōrum et ego auribus parturiēbam quidquid sentiēbam. hinc satis ēlūcet maiōrem habēre vim ad discendā ista līberam cūriōsitātem

---

adlūdō, -ere, -sī: speak playfully, jest, 1
adrīdeō, -ēre, -rīsī: smile/laugh at, 1
(anim)advertō, -ere, -tī, adversum: turn (the mind) to, pay attention, *notice*, 2
aliquandō: sometimes, at some time, 2
blandīmentum, -ī n.: flattery, charm, 1
concipiō, -ere, -cēpī: receive, take in, *subst. of pass. part.* things conceived, ideas, 2
cruciātus, -ūs m.: torture, torment, 1
cūriōsitās, -ātis f.: curiosity, 2
doceō, -ēre, -uī, -ctum: teach, tell, 4
ēlūceō, -ēre, -xī: shine out; is clear, 1
fābulōsus, -a, -um: fantastical, mythical, 1
hinc: from here, hence, 3
īnstō, -āre, -stitī: stand, press (on), put pressure on, insist, 2
inter: between, among (acc.), 4
iocus, ī m. (pl. ioca n.): joke, 1
laetitia, -ae f.: happiness, joy, 1
Latīnus, -a, -um: Latin, 2
līber lībera līberum: free, 3
metus, -ūs f.: dread, fear, 2
nārrātiō, -iōnis f.: narrative, 1
nōscō, -ere, nōvī, nōtum: know (how) 4
nūtrīx, nūtrīcis f.: nurse, 3
onus, oneris n.: burden, load, freight, 1
pariō, -ere, peperī, partum: produce, bear, 2
parturiō, -īre : be in labor, 2
poena, -ae, f.: punishment, 3
poenālis, -e: of punishment, penal, punitive, 3
saevus, -a, -um: savage, fierce, 1
satis: enough, sufficient, 4
terror, terrōris m.: terror, fright, 1
ūllus, -a, -um: any, 3
vehementer: strongly, violently, 1
vīs, (vīs), f.: force, power, violence, 1

21 **nārrātiōnum:** subj. gen.
22 **nōveram... nōssem** (= *nōvissem* A&G 181a)**... nōveram**; pf. system forms with pr. system meanings
saevīs terrōribus... poenīs: abls. of means
ut nōssem īnstābātur: *it was being insisted that I know*; subst. cl. with pass. verb (A&G 566); the **ut**-cl. is the subj. of the verb.
23 **latīna (verba)**
25 **nūtrīcum**: f. gen. pl. of third declension
adrīdentium...adlūdentium...urgentium subj. gen. pl. pr. act. subst. parts.
26 **cum urgēret:** causal **cum**-cl. (A&G 549)
27 **ad parienda concepta sua:** gerundive functioning as a gerund in the num. and gen. of its obj. Before the change it would have been *pariendum concepta* (A&G 503)
nōn possem, nisi... didicissem: *which I could not (now) do, if I had not (previously) learned*; mixed CTF
28 **docentibus... loquentibus**: abl. of agent pl. pr. act. subst. parts.
30 **ista**= *haec*
ēlūcet cūriōsitātem habēre vim: *it is clear that curiosity has power*; acc./inf. in indirect statement

quam meticulōsam necessitātem. sed illīus flūxum haec restringit lēgibus tuīs, deus, lēgibus tuīs ā magistrōrum ferulīs usque ad temptātiōnēs martyrum, valentibus lēgibus tuīs miscēre salūbrēs amāritūdinēs revocantēs nōs ad tē ā iūcunditāte pestiferā quā recessimus ā tē.

1.15.24 exaudī, domine, dēprecātiōnem meam, nē dēficiat anima mea sub disciplīnā tuā neque dēficiam in cōnfitendō tibi miserātiōnēs tuās, quibus ēruistī mē ab omnibus viīs meīs pessimīs, ut dulcēscās mihi super omnēs sēductiōnēs quās sequēbar, et amem tē validissimē, et amplexer manum tuam tōtīs praecordiīs meīs, et

---

amāritūdō, -inis f.: bitterness, 1
amplexor, -ārī, -ātus sum: dep. embrace, 1
dēficiō, -ere, -fēcī, -fectum: fail, lose heart 3
dēprecātiō, -ōnis f.: prayer (to avert), 1
disciplīna, -ae f.: training, instruction, 3
dulcēscō, -ere, -cuī: become sweet, 1
ēruō, -ere, -ī, ērutum: dig up, tear out, 3
exaudiō, -īre, -īvī, -ītum hear plainly, really hear, hear out; hear with compassion, 4
ferula, -ae f.: reed, whip, rod, 2
flūxus, -a, -um: pliable; fleeting, perishable, 1
iūcunditās, -ātis f.: pleasantness, 1
manus, -ūs f.: hand, 1
martyr martyris m./f.: martyr, 1
meticulōsus, -a, -um: full of fear, 1
misceō, -ēre, -uī, mīxtum: mix, mingle, 1
miserātiō, -ōnis f.: compassion, 3
necessitās, -tātis f.: necessity, need, 1
neque: and not; neither…nor, 2
pessimus, -a, -um: worst, very bad, 1
pestiferus, -a, -um: plague-bearing, 1
praecordia, -ōrum n.: heart, abdoman, 1
recēdō, -ere, -cessī: go back, withdraw, 2
restringō, -ere, -xī, -ctum: tie back, restrain 1
revocō (1): call back, summon back, 1
salūber, -bris, -bre: healthy, 1
sēductiō, -ōnis f.: a leading astray, 1
sequor, -ī, secūtus: follow, pursue; chase; seek, 4
sub: under (abl.), 1
super: above, upon; beyond, more than, 3
temptātiō, -ōnis f.: trial, temptation, 3
usque: (all the way) up to, continuously, 4
valeō, -ēre, uī: be strong, fare well, be able (inf), 3
validus, -a, -um: healthy, vigorous, strong, 1

1 **meticulōsam**: occurs two times in Latin with this meaning of fearful (O'Donnell)
illīus (cūriositātis)… haec (necessitās) revocantēs = *quae revocant nōs…*
necessitātem… sēductiōnēs: six abstract nouns on this page: a mark of IL (C&M 57)
lēgibus tuīs… lēgibus tuīs… lēgibus tuīs: repetition and asyndeton are common features of A.'s outbursts of prayer and praise: cf. *laudes tuae* p. 46

6 **dēprecātiōnem… nē dēficiat… neque dēficiam**… *prayer that… not fail… and that I not fail…*;An *ut*-clause following verbs of will and desire (indir. comm.) take the subj.

7 **sub disciplīna tuā**: an IL idiom (C&M 88c)
in confitendō…: "But every time Augustine uses the word 'confiteri' it means a renewed turning toward God" (Knauer)

8 **ēruistī**: *you have rescued*; must be *present* perfect to match the sequence of tenses.
pessimīs "All superlative force seems to have gone out of the word" (G&M)

9 **ut dulcēscās… amem… amplexer…**: subjs. in purp. cl. (A&G 529)
dulcēscās: the –**sc** in the stem indicates an inceptive or inchoative sense (A&G 263.1)
super omnēs: *more than all*; a IL usage (C&M 88d 2-3)

ēruās mē ab omnī temptātiōne usque in fīnem. ecce enim tū, domine, rēx meus et deus meus, tibi serviat quidquid ūtile puer didicī, tibi serviat quod loquor et scrībō et lēgō et numerō, quoniam cum vāna discerem tū disciplīnam dabās mihi, et in eīs vānīs peccāta dēlectātiōnum meārum dīmīsistī mihi. didicī enim in eīs multa verba ūtilia, sed et in rēbus nōn vānīs discī possunt, et ea via tūta est in quā puerī ambulārent.

1.16.25 sed vae tibi, flūmen mōris hūmānī! quis resistet tibi? quamdiū nōn siccāberis? quousque volvēs Ēvae fīliōs in mare magnum et formīdulōsum, quod vix trānseunt quī lignum

---

ambulō (1): walk, 2
dēlectātiō, -ōnis f.: delight, enjoyment, 3
dīmittō, -ere, -mīsī, -missus: send (away), 2
disciplīna, -ae f.: training, instruction, 3
ēruō, -ere, -ī, ērutum: dig up, tear out, 3
Ēva, -ae f.: Eve, the first woman, 1
fīnis, -is m./f.: end, border; territory, 2
flūmen, -inis n.: river, stream, 2
formīdulōsus, -a, -um: dreadful, formidable 1
hūmānus, -a, -um: human, 4
lignum, -ī n.: wood, ship, 1
mare, maris n.: sea, 1
mōs, mōris m.: custom, way; character, 3
numerus, -ī m.: number, count, multitude, 2
quamdiū: how long?; as long as, 1
quousque: until what time, till when, 1
resistō, -ere, -stitī: resist, oppose (dat) 2
rēx, rēgis m.: king; *adj.* ruling, royal, 4
siccō (1): dry (up), 1
temptātiō, -ōnis f.: trial, temptation, 3
tūtus, -a, -um: safe, secure, guarded, 2
usque: (all the way) up to, continuously, 4
ūtilis, -e: useful, 3
vae: woe, 3
vix: with difficulty, with effort, scarcely, 1
volvō, -ere, volvī, volūtus: turn over, 1

11 **(ut) ēruās**: purp. cl. continued from previous pg. "[**eruas** is] Almost always in conf. of God's rescuing hand."
12 **tibi serviat quidquid ūtile puer didicī**: *may whatever I learned as a boy serve you*; **quidquid... didicī** is subj. of **serviat**, which is juss. subj. (A&G 439)
13 **serviat quod**: *may the fact that I...*; 'fact-that' **quod** cl. as subj. of **serviat.**
14 **cum vāna discerem**: conc. **cum**-cl.
15 **mihi**: ethical dat. (A&G 380) or perhaps dat. of separation (381). In CL we would have a/ab or *ex* + *abl.*, but A. seems to want to indicate here the *personal benefit* of the forgiveness for him.
17 **ambulārent**: *might walk*; pot. subj.
19 **siccāberis**: 2 sg. ft. pf. ind.
volvēs: 2 sg. ft. act. ind. of 3rd conj.s
20 **lignum**: "the way is broken up by the 'floods of this life, and you will not cross it to the fatherland, unless carried by a *lignum*... believe in the cross and you will be able to cross over" (G&M).
o flumen : "In the ensuing lines -

Quoniam, Quod, Quia (A&G 539-40; 572)

1. **In CL *quod* and *quia*** take the subjunctive when they represent the thoughts other than the speaker, the indicative when the thoughts of the speaker: this rule is generally followed by A.
2. **In IL *quia* slowly replaced *quod*** as the normal (subordinating) conjunction (cf. p. 9, l. 28)
3. **As an explanatory, "fact that" clause, the *quod*-clause** may be the subject or object of the verb, or in apposition to a noun or neut. pronoun, as above it is the subject. of the verb **serviat**
4. **In CL we never have *quod* or *quia*** in indirect discourse (rather the acc./inf. construction), but in A., as in most late Latin, they are frequent, accompanied by subjunctive or indicative according to rule 1 above.

cōnscenderint? nōnne ego in tē lēgī et tonantem Iovem et adulterantem? et ūtique nōn posset haec duo, sed āctum est ut habēret auctōritātem ad imitandum vērum adulterium lēnōcinante falsō tonitrū. quis autem paenulātōrum magistrōrum audit aure sōbriā ex eōdem pulvere hominem clāmantem et dīcentem: 'fingēbat haec Homērus et hūmāna ad deōs trānsferēbat: dīvīna māllem ad nōs'? sed vērius dīcitur quod fingēbat haec quidem ille, sed hominibus flāgitiōsīs dīvīna tribuendō, nē flāgitia flāgitia putārentur et ut, quisquis ea fēcisset, nōn hominēs perditōs sed caelestēs deōs vidērētur imitātus.

---

adulterium, -ī n.: adultery, 1
adulterō (1): commit adultery, 1
auctōritās, -tātis f.: authority, clout, 3
caelestis, -e: celestial, heavenly, 2
cōnscendō, -ere, -ndī, -nsum: mount, 1
dīvīnus, -a, -um: divine, 2
duo, duae, duo: two, 4
fingō, -ere, finxī, fictum: make up, fashion, 2
flāgitiōsus, -a, -um: disgraceful, shameful, 1
flāgitium, -ī n.: disgraceful/shameful act, 2
Homērus, ī m.: Homer, 2
hūmānus, -a, -um: human, 4
imitor, -ārī, imitātum: imitate, copy, 4
Iuppiter, Iovis m.: Jupiter, 3
lēnōcinor, -ārī, -ātus: pander, flatter, 1
mālō, mālle, maluī: prefer, 1
paenulātus, -a, -um: cloak-wearing, 1
perdō, -ere, -didī, -ditus: lose, ruin, 2
pulvis, pulveris m.: dust, 1
putō (1): think, consider, 2
quidem: indeed, in fact, assuredly, certainly, 3
sōbrius, -a, -um: sober, moderate, 2
tonitrus, -ūs m.: thunder, 1
tonō (1): thunder, 1
trānsferō, ferre, tulī, lātum: carry across; impute to, 1
tribuō, -ere, -uī, tribūtum: distribute, dispose, bestow, assign, 2

21 - metaphor and reality jostle one another in a very awkward fashion" (G&M)
cōnscenderint: 3 pl. fut. pf. indic.: the proceeding futs. suggest it is not pf. subj.
tē (flūmen moris humānī):
et... et: *both... and...*

22 **(Iuppiter) nōn posset:** impf. pot. subj.
āctum est ut adulterium habēret auctōritātem ad... : *it was done so that adultery might have authority for...*

23 **habēret**: 3 sg. impf. act. subj. in sec. seq. purp. cl.
ad imitandum: **ad**+ gerund for purp. (A&G 506)
lēnōcinante falsō tonitrū: abl. abs.

24 **quis autem paenulātōrum magistrōrum**: part. gen. (A&G 346)
paenulātōrum: see a dict. or O'Donnell for a full explanation of this word.
aure sōbriā: abl. of manner: the auditory analog to the idiom *aequō animō*

25 **māllem (illum) dīvīna ad nōs trānsferre**: *I'd prefer that...*; implied acc. and inf. construction.

27 **dīcitur quod**: instead of CL's indirect statement with acc./inf. construction
ille: CL's 'that famous'

28 **dīvīna tribuendō**: normally the abl. gerund does not take a direct object but is changed into a gerundive (A&G 503a note 1; cf. G&L 427 note 3). Cf. p. 40. l. 7.
nē... putārentur... ut... vidērētur: neg. and pos. purp. cls. with impf. subjs.
quisquis ea fēcisset = *sī quis...* ; the protasis of a past CTF.

30 **imitātus (esse)**: pf. pass. compl. inf. with *vidērī* (A&G 456)

1.16.26 et tamen, ō flūmen Tartareum, iactantur in tē fīliī hominum cum mercēdibus, ut haec discant, et magna rēs agitur cum hōc agitur pūblicē in forō, in cōnspectū lēgum suprā mercēdem salāria dēcernentium, et saxa tua percutis et sonās dīcēns: 'hinc verba discuntur, hinc adquīritur ēloquentia, rēbus persuādendīs sententiīsque explicandīs maximē necessāria.' ita vērō nōn cognōscerēmus verba haec, 'imbrem aureum' et 'gremium' et 'fūcum' et 'templa caelī' et alia verba quae in eō locō scrīpta sunt, nisi Terentius indūceret nēquam adulēscentem prōpōnentem sibi Iovem ad exemplum stuprī, dum spectat tabulam

---

adquīrō, -ere, -quīsīvī: seek in addition, 1
adulēscens, -ntis m./f.: youth, 1
aureus, -a, -um: golden, 2
cognōscō, -ere, -nōvī, -nitum: learn, know, 1
cōnspectus, -ūs m.: look, sight, view, 2
dēcernō, -ere, -crēvī: decide, judge; decree, 1
dum: while, as long as, until, 2
ēloquentia, -ae f.: eloquence, 2
exemplum, -ī n.: example, 1,
explicō (1): unfold; explain, 1
flūmen, -inis n.: river, stream, 2
forum, -ī n.: forum, 1
fūcus, -ī m.: disguise; a seaweed, 2
gremium, -iī n.: lap, bosom, 2
hinc: from here, hence, 3
iactō (1): throw, toss back and forth, 2
imber, imbris m.: rain, 2
indūcō, -ere, -dūxī: bring or lead into, 1
Iuppiter, Iovis m.: Jupiter, 3
locus -ī m. (pl. loca): place, region, 4
maximē: exspecially, most greatly, 1
mercēs, mercēdis f.: pay, wages, 2
necessārius, -a, -um: necessary, needful, 1
nēquam (indecl.): useless, good for nothing
ō: oh (in exclamation), 2
percutiō, -ere, -cussī: strike, 4
persuādeō, -ēre, -suāsī: persuade, *argue*, 1
pūblicus, -a, -um: public, common, 1
salārium, -ī n.: stipend, salary, 1
saxum, -ī n.: rock, 1
sententia, -ae f.: thought, (court) sentence, 3
sonō (1): sound, resound, echo, 4
spectō (1): watch, look at, 2
stuprum, -ī n.: (an act of) debauchery, 1
suprā: above, over (and beyond), on the top, 2
tabula, -ae f.: wooden board, tablet, 1
Tartareus, -a, -um: of Tartarus; Tartarean, 1
templum, -ī n.: temple, 2
Terentius, -ī m.: Terence, Roman playright, wrote his plays c. 100 b.c.

2 **ut haec discant:** pr. act. subj. in purp. cl.
cum mercēdibus: abl. of accompaniment takes **cum**.
magna rēs agitur: *a great big commotion occurs.*

3 **in cōnspectū:** an IL turn of phrase (C&M 88b 1) and asyndeton (lack of a connective)
dēcernentium: gen. f. pl. pr. act. part.

5 **hinc... hinc**: *this is why* (Clark)
rēbus persuādendīs sententiīsque explicandīs: *for arguing cases and explaining (court) opinions.*

6 **necessaria** takes the dat. of purp. here, fitting to the legal context (A&G 505b)

7 **cognōscerēmus... indūceret**: impf. subjs. instead of plpfs. in a past CTF, perhaps for the sake of vividness (C&M 78b)

10 **prōpōnentem**: acc. sg. pr. act. subst. part
ad exemplum stuprī: *as an example of debauchery*; **ad** + acc. to express purpose instead of a double dative (C&M 86a.2);
stuprī is an appositional gen. (A&G 343d), which is simply a variation of the poss. gen.

quandam pictam in pariete ubi inerat pictūra haec, Iovem quō pactō Danaē mīsisse aiunt in gremium quondam imbrem aureum, fūcum factum mulierī? et vidē quemadmodum sē concitat ad libīdinem quasi caelestī magisteriō: 'at quem deum! inquit quī templa caelī summō sonitū concutit. ego homunciō id nōn facerem? ego vērō illud fēcī ac libēns.' nōn omnīnō per hanc turpitūdinem verba ista commodius discuntur, sed per haec verba turpitūdō ista cōnfīdentius perpetrātur. nōn accūsō verba quasi vāsa ēlēcta atque pretiōsa, sed vīnum errōris quod in eīs nōbīs propīnābātur ab ēbriīs doctōribus, et nisi biberēmus caedēbāmur,

---

accūsō (1): accuse, blame, 1
aiō: say, 2
aureus, -a, -um: golden, 2
bibō, -ere, bibī: drink, 1
caedō, -ere, cecīdī, caesus: kill, cut down, 1
caelestis, -e: celestial, heavenly, 2
commodus, -a, -um: convenient, beneficial
concitō (1): stir up, incite, impel, 1
concutiō, -ere, -cussī: strike, 1
cōnfīdēns, -entis: bold, confident, 1
Danaē, -ēs f.: Danae, 1
doctor, -ōris m.: instructor, 1
ēbrius, -a, -um: drunk, inebriated, 1
ēligō, -ere, -ī, ēlēctus: pick out, choose, 2
fūcus, -ī m.: dye; disguise, pretense, deceit, 2
gremium, -iī n.: lap, bosom, 2
homunciō, -ōnis m.: little man, manikin, 1
imber, imbris m.: rain, 2
inquam, inquis, inquit: say, 2
insum, -esse, -fuī: be in, 1
Iuppiter, Iovis m.: Jupiter, 3
libet, libuit: it is pleasing (impers.), 2
libīdō, libidinis f.: passion, desire, lust, 2
magisterium, -ī n.: (public) office, 1
mittō, -ere, -mīsī, -missus: send, let go, 1
mulier, mulieris f.: woman, 1
omnīnō: altogether, (strengthens neg.) *at all* 4
pactum, -ī n.: pact, agreement, 4
pariēs, parietis m.: wall, 1
perpetrō, -āre: accomplish, 1
pictūra, -ae f.: painting, picture, 1
pingō, -ere, pīnxī, pictus: paint, 1
pretiōsus, -a, -um: expensive, costly, 1
propīnō (1): drink to one's health, 1
quemadmodum: in what manner, how, 2
quīdam, quae-, quid-: a certain, 3
quondam: formerly, once, 1
sonitus, -ī m.: sound, noise, clang, 2
templum, -ī n.: temple, 2
turpitūdō, -inis f.: disgrace, turpitude, 3
vās, vāsis n.: vessel, 2
vīnum, vīnī n.: wine, 1

11 **quō pactō aiunt Iovem mīsisse quondam imbrem aureum in gremium Danaē** : acc. inf. construction in relative clause.
13 **(illum vēnisse) fūcum factum mulierī**: *that he (Jove) came to play a trick on the woman*; **factum** is an acc. sup. with a verb of motion to show purp. (A&G 509); it takes **fūcum** as its obj.; the *vēnisse* comes from a part of Terence not quoted by A. **concitat**: normally we would expect *-et* in an indir. quest. (A&G 330; 575c).
14 **ad... ad** + acc. and the dat. are parallel. **at quem deum!**: *but what a god!* excl. acc. **inquit**: always parenthetical (A&G 599c)
16 **libēns**: *with pleasure*; nom. s. pr. act. part.
18 **vāsa** : "The apparent container is really the thing permeated, underpinned, and itself contained by the divine." (O'Donnell) Cf. with p. 4
19 **errōris**: is an appos. gen. (A&G 343d)
20 **et (ā eīs) nisi biberēmus caedēbāmur**: past gen. cond. with impf. subj. instead of the normal plpf. indic. of CL (A&G 514.D.2b)

nec appellāre ad aliquem iūdicem sōbrium licēbat. et tamen ego, deus meus, in cuius cōnspectū iam sēcūra est recordātiō mea, libenter haec didicī, et eīs dēlectābar miser, et ob hōc bonae speī puer appellābar.

1.17.27 sine mē, deus meus, dīcere aliquid et dē ingeniō meō, mūnere tuō, in quibus ā mē dēlīrāmentīs atterēbātur. prōpōnēbātur enim mihi negōtium, animae meae satis inquiētum praemiō laudis et dēdecoris vel plāgārum metū, ut dīcerem verba Iūnōnis īrāscentis et dolentis quod nōn posset Ītaliā Teucrōrum āvertere rēgem, quae numquam Iūnōnem dīxisse audieram. Sed

---

appellō (1): call (by name), name; appeal 3
atterō, -ere, -ivī: wear down; weaken; waste 1
āvertō, -ere, -vertī: turn away/aside, 1
cōnspectus, -ūs m.: look, sight, view, 2
dēdecus, -oris f.: dishonor, shame; crime, 1
dēlīrāmentum, -ī n.: nonsensical/absurd action, 1
doleō, -ēre, -uī: grieve, feel pain, 4
ingenium, -ī n.: intellect, talent; character, 3
inquiētus, -a, -um: restless, disturbed; disquieting 2
īrāscor, -ī, īrātus sum: become or be angry, 3
Ītalia, -ae f.: Italy, 1
iūdex, iūdicis m.: judge, juror, 2
Iūnō, -ōnis m.: Juno, 2
laus, laudis f.: praise, adulation, 4
libenter: gladly, willingly, 2
licet, -ēre, -uit: is allowed, permitted, 2
metus, -ūs f.: dread, fear, 2
mūnus, -eris n.: service, duty; gift, 1
negōtium, iī n.: task, business, 2
ob: on account of (*acc.*), 1
plāga, -ae f.: blow, 2
praemium, -ī n.: reward, prize, 1
recordātiō, -ōnis f.: recollection, 1
rēx, rēgis m.: king; *adj.* ruling, royal, 4
satis: enough, sufficient, 4
sēcūrus, -a, -um: free from care, 2
sōbrius, -a, -um: sober, moderate, 2
spēs, -ēī f.: hope, expectation, 1
Teucrī, -ōrum m.: Trojans (descendents of Teucer), 1

21 **nec licēbat appellāre**: *nor was appealing permitted*; *licet* may take 1) subj. without *ut*, 2) the simple inf. subj. (as here), 3) the inf. and subj. acc. or 4) the dat. and inf. (A&G 565 n. 2)

23 **eīs dēlectābar: delectō** in the pass. takes an abl. of means, but may here, like *fruor* or *utor* be being used in a middle sense, e.g., *I delighted myself in them* (C&M 77) **bonae speī puer**: gen. of quality expresses essential characteristics in contrast to the abl. of quality, though this distinction is not always observed (A&G 545 n.)

26 **in quibus ā mē dēlīrāmentīs**: hyperbaton; perhaps an instance of instrumental **in** (C&M 88b.4) but see O'Donnell.

27 **praemiō... metū**: abls. of cause with **inquietum**, which is in app. to **negōtium.**

28 **negōtium... ut dīcerem**: *the task that I speak...*; an *ut*-clause following verbs of will and desire (indir. comm.) takes the subj. (A&G 563) "so it happens that he learns to discern his own feelings in attempting to express those of a stranger." Boissier in (G&M)

29 **quod nōn posset:** either subj. to impute disbelief (A&G 540 n. 1) or perhaps representing the deliberation of Juno: *cum Iuno, aeternum servans sub pectore volnus, // haec secum: 'Mene incepto desistere victam, // nec posse Italia Teucrorum avertere regem?* (Aen.1.36-38)

figmentōrum poēticōrum vestīgia errantēs sequī cōgēbāmur, et tāle aliquid dīcere solūtīs verbīs quāle poēta dīxisset versibus. et ille dīcēbat laudābilius in quō prō dignitāte adumbrātae persōnae īrae ac dolōris similior affectus ēminēbat, verbīs sententiās congruenter vestientibus. ut quid mihi illud, ō vēra vīta, deus meus, quod mihi recitantī adclāmābātur prae multīs coaetāneīs et conlēctōribus meīs? nōnne ecce illa omnia fūmus et ventus? itane aliud nōn erat ubi exercērētur ingenium et lingua mea? laudēs tuae, domine, laudēs tuae per scrīptūrās tuās suspenderent palmitem cordis meī, et nōn raperētur per inānia nūgārum turpis praeda volātilibus. Nōn

---

adclāmō (1): call to, shout at, 1
adumbrō (1): obscure, shade over, 1
coaetāneus, -a, -um: contemporary, 1
congruēns, -entis: agreeing, fitting 2
conlēctor, -ōris m.: fellow-student, 1
dignitās, -tātis f.: worth, worthiness, 2
dolor, -ōris m.: grief, pain, 4
ēmineō, -ēre, -uī: stand out, 1
errō (1): wander, 1
exerceō, -ēre, -uī, -ercitum: exercise, 1
figmentum, -ī n.: picture, image; creation; figment, act of (vain) imagination, 2
fūmus, -ī m.: smoke, 1
inānis, is: empty; vain, groundless, 2
ingenium, -ī n.: intellect, talent; character, 3
īra, īrae f.: anger, 1
laudābilis, -e: worthy of praise, laudable, 3
laus, laudis f.: praise, adulation, 4
lingua, ae f.: tongue, language, 4
nūgae, -ārum f.: nonsense, trifles, jokes, 2
palmes, -itis m.: vine, bough, branch, 1
persōna, -ae f.: an actor's mask; role, 1
poēta, -ae m.: poet, 2
poēticus, -a, -um: relating to poet(ry), 2
prae: because of, for (acc); before (abl), 1
praeda, -ae f.: plunder, spoils, cattle, 1
quālis, -e: what sort?, 2
rapiō, -ere, -uī, raptum: snatch, seize, 1
recitō (1): recite, read aloud, 1
scrīptūra, -ae f.: writing, 1
sententia, -ae f.: thought, (court) sentence, 3
sequor, -ī, secūtus: follow, pursue; chase; seek, 4
similis, -e: similar to, like (dat.), 3
solūtus, -a, -um : unbound, free, 1
suspendō, -ere, -pendī: hang up; support, 1
turpis, -e: ugly, shameful, 1
ventus, -ī m.: wind, 1
versus, -ūs m.: verse, line of poetry, 1
vestīgium, -iī n.: track, foot-print, trace, 3
vestiō, -īre, -iī: clothe, dress, 1
volātilis, -e: fleeting, able to fly; subst.: bird, 1

1 **sequī... dīcere**: compl. infs. with *cogō* (A&G 456) ; **tāle... quāle**: *of such (a sort)... of what (sort)*

2 **solūtīs verbīs**: *in prose*; abl. of manner **dīxisset**: 3 s. plpf. act. subj. in indir. quest. sec. sequ. (A&G 330)

5 **ut quid**: *why?*; an IL construction influenced by translations of the Bible.

6 **coaetāneīs et conlēctōribus**: first appearance of the latter in Latin (O'Donnell) cf. *conlactaneus* (p. 18) *condoctor* (p. 26).

8 **ubi exercērētur ingenium**: **ubi** with impf. subj. indicates a past state of things (A&G 543a); **exercērētur** takes the number of the nearest subj. **laudēs tuae... laudēs**: cf. *tuis legibus* p. 40

9 **suspenderent... nōn raperētur**: *ought to have supported... and then it would not have been snatched*; nearly a past CTF but with impf. subjs. (C&M 78b). **raperētur** is attracted into the number of **praeda**,

10 **turpis praeda**: predicative appos. to implied subj. **palmitēs cordis**

enim ūnō modo sacrificātur trānsgressōribus angelīs.

1.18.28 quid autem mīrum, quod in vānitātēs ita ferēbar et ā tē, deus meus, ībam forās, quandō mihi imitandī prōpōnēbantur hominēs quī aliqua facta sua nōn mala, sī cum barbarismō aut soloecismō ēnūntiārent, reprehēnsī cōnfundēbantur, sī autem libīdinēs suās integrīs et rīte cōnsequentibus verbīs cōpiōsē ōrnātēque narrārent, laudātī glōriābantur? vidēs haec, domine, et tacēs, longanimis et multum misericors et vērāx. numquid semper tacēbis? et nunc ēruīs dē hōc immānissimō profundō quaererentem tē animam et sitientem dēlectātiōnēs tuās, et cuius cor dīcit tibi,

---

angelus, -ī m.: messenger, angel, 1
barbarismus, -ī m.: an impropriety of speech, barbarism, 2
cōnfundō, -ere -fūdī, -fūsus: pour together, 1
cōnsequor, -ī, secūtus: follow, pursue, 1
cōpiōsus, -a, -um: abundant, plentiful, 2
dēlectātiō, -ōnis f.: delight, enjoyment, 3
ēnūntiō (1): announce, disclose, 3
eō, īre, iī/īvī, itum: go, 3
ēruō, -ere, -ī, ērutum: dig up, tear out, 3
ferō, ferre, tulī, lātus: carry, bear, endure, 3
forās: out of doors; outside; outward, 1
glōrior, -ārī, -ātus sum: glorify, boast, 1
imitor, -ārī, imitātum: imitate, copy, 4
immānis, -e: immense, huge, 2
integer, -gra, -grum: untouched, unhurt, 1
libīdō, libidinis f.: passion, desire, lust, 2
longanimis, -e: long-suffering, patient, 1
mīrus, -a, -um: wonderful, amazing, 1
misericors, -ordis: compassionate, merciful, 4
narrō (1): narrate, relate, 1
numquid: *surely...not?* (emphatic num), 1
ōrnātē: ornately, richly, elaborately, 1
profundus, -a, -um: deep
quandō: when, since, 3
rītē: duly, fitly, 1
sacrificō (1): sacrifice, 1
semper: always, ever, forever, 4
sitiēns, sitientis: thirsty, 1
soloecismus, -ī m.: a grammatical error, solecism, 1
taceō, -ēre, -uī, -itum: be silent, 3
trānsgressor, -ōris m.: transgressor, *transgressing*, 1
vānitās, -ātis f.: emptiness; fickleness, folly, 4
vērāx, -ācis : veracious, speaking truly, 1

11 **sacrificātur**: A. is fond of impersonal passives (C&M 77)
trānsgressōribus: the use of substantives as an adj. is not normal in CL, but becomes more so in IL (C&M 64); *generally* only the substantives that indicate agency become adjs. (A&G 236a)..

12 **quid autem (est) mīrum, quod...**: *why is is baffling that...* ; 'fact-that' **quod** cl. as subj. of implied *erat* (A&G 572)
hominēs quī, reprehēnsī cōnfundēbantur sī ēnūntiārent (et quī) laudātī glōriābantur sī narrārent, mihi prōpōnēbantur: proof that A. could write a good period when he wanted: but, "A . is *not* a master of the period to the same extent as of the phrase" (G&M on 1.9.15)
sī ēnūntiārent... sī narrārent: past gen. conds. with impf. subj. instead of the normal plpf. indic. of CL (A&G 514.D.2b)

13 **imitandī prōpōnēbantur hominēs**: *there were being held out to me men to be imitated* (A&G 500)

19 **et nunc**: *even now*: referring retrospectively to how God was rescuing A. though he couldn't tell it--or perhaps stating a universal truth.
quaererentem... sitientem: acc. s. f. pr. act. part. modifying *anima* and taking each one a direct object.

'quaesīvī vultum tuum.' vultum tuum, domine, requīram: nam longē ā vultū tuō in affectū tenebrōsō. nōn enim pedibus aut ā spatiīs locōrum ītur abs tē aut redītur ad tē, aut vērō fīlius ille tuus minor equōs vel currūs vel nāvēs quaesīvit, aut āvolāvit pinnā vīsibilī, aut mōtō poplite iter ēgit, ut in longinquā regiōne vīvēns prōdige dissipāret quod dederās proficīscentī, dulcis pater quia dederās, et egēnō redeuntī dulcior: in affectū ergō libīdinōsō, id enim est tenebrōsō, atque id est longē ā vultū tuō.

1.18.29 vidē, domine deus, et patienter, ut vidēs, vidē quōmodo dīligenter observent fīliī hominum pacta litterārum et syllabārum

---

āvolō (1): fly away, 1
currus, -ūs m.: chariot, cart, 1
dīligēns (dīligentis): careful, diligent, 1
dissipō (1): scatter, disperse, 2
dulcis, -e: sweet, pleasant, 4
egēnus, -a, -um: needy, in want
eō, īre, iī/īvī, itum: go, 3
equus, -ī m.: horse, 2
iter, itineris n.: way, road, journey, 1
libīdō, libidinis f.: passion, desire, lust, 2
locus -ī m. (pl. loca): place, region, 4
longē: far, at a distant, 2
longinquus, -a, -um: distant, remote, far off, 1
moveō, -ēre, mōvī, mōtum: move, 2
nāvis, -is f.: ship, 1
observō (1): watch, observe, attend to, 2
pactum, -ī n.: pact, agreement, 4
patior, -ī, passus: suffer, endure; allow, 4
pēs, pedis m.: foot, 1
pinna, -ae f.: feather, wing; quill, 1
poples, -itis m.: knee, back part of the knee; hamstring, 1
prōdigus, -a, -um: wasteful, lavish, 1
proficīscor, -ī, -fectus: set out, depart, 1
quōmodo: how, in what way, 4
redeō, -īre, -īvī: go back, return, 2
regiō, -ōnis f.: region, district, 1
requīrō, -ere: seek out, ask, inquire, 2
spatium, -iī n.: space, span, extent, 1
syllaba, -ae f.: syllabus, 2
tenebrōsus, -a, -um: dark, murky, 2
vīsibilis, -e: visible, 1

21 **requīram**: 1 s. fut. act. indic.
22 **longē (eram)**_
nōn... aut... aut... aut... aut... aut = **nec... nec...** *etc.*
23 **ītur... redītur** : impersonal passives (C&M 77) ; "The thought and expression here are alike coloured by Neo-Platonism... A. has here fused together the parable of the Prodigal Son and a passage from Plotinus" (G&M)
25 **mōtō poplite**: *by bending the knee*; *ab urpe condita* construction (A&G 497)
ut... dissipāret: *so that he might* ; impf. subj. sec. seq. in purp. cl. (A&G 531)
26 **(eī) proficīscentī... redeuntī**: *to him as he set out... to him as he returned*; dat. s. m. pr. act. subst. parts.
dulcis (tu) pater... dulcior (tu eras)
27 **id est... id est**: *that is... that is*; whence "i.e." in modern academic writing.
28 **vidē...ut vidēs, vidē**: *as you in fact do see*; again here repetition and anacolouthon in direct address to God, see *tuis legibus* p. 40 or *laudes tuae* p. 46
30 **observent** : subj. in indir. quest.
litterārum et syllabārum : appositional gens. (A&G 343d), which is simply a variation of the poss. gen.

accepta ā priōribus locūtōribus, et ā tē accepta aeterna pacta perpetuae salūtis neglegant, ut quī illa sonōrum vetera placita teneat aut doceat, sī contrā disciplīnam grammaticam sine adspīrātiōne prīmae syllabae hominem dīxerit, magis displiceat hominibus quam sī contrā tua praecepta hominem ōderit, cum sit homō. quasi vērō quemlibet inimīcum hominem perniciōsius sentiat quam ipsum odium quō in eum inrītātur, aut vastet quisquam persequendō alium gravius quam cor suum vastat inimīcandō. et certē nōn est interior litterārum scientia quam scrīpta cōnscientia, id sē alterī facere quod nōlit patī. quam tū

---

accipiō -ere -cēpī -ceptum: receive, accept, 4
adspīrātiō, -ōnis f.: exhalation; aspiration, 1
aeternus, -a, -um: everlasting, eternal, 2
alter, -era, -erum: other (of two), 2
certus, -a, -um: certain, reliable,, sure, 4
cōnscientia, -ae f.: consciousness, conscience
contrā: opposite, facing, *against* (acc.) 3
disciplīna, -ae f.: training, instruction, 3
displiceō, -ere, -uī: displease, 2
doceō, -ēre, -uī, -ctum: teach, tell, 4
gravis, -e: heavy, serious, important, 2
inimīcō (1): make enemies; cherish hostile feelings, be hostile, 1
inimīcus, -a, -um: unfriendly, 2
inrītō (1): irritate, exasperate
interior, -ius: inner, interior, 2
locūtor, -ōris m.: a speaker, 1
neglegō, ere, -lēxī, neglēctum: neglect, 1
odium, -iī n.: hatred, 2
pactum, -ī n.: pact, agreement, 4
patior, -ī, passus: suffer, endure; allow, 4
perniciōsus, -a, -um: destructive, ruinous, 2
perpetuus, -a, -um: perpetual, everlasting, 1
persequor, -sequī, -secūtus: persecute, 1
placeō, -ēre, -uī, placitum: please, be pleasing, pf. part. subst.: something agreed upon, prescription, principle, 3
praecipiō, -ere, -cēpī, -ceptum: order, take, 2
prior, prius: before, earlier (comp. prīmus), 4
quīlibet, quae- quod-: whoever or whatever you please; anyone, anything, 2
scientia, -ae f.: knowledge, wisdom, 1
sonus, -ī m.: sound, 2
syllaba, -ae f.: syllabus, 2
teneō, -ere, tenuī, tentum: hold, keep, *maintain*, 3
vastō (1): lay waste, 2
vetus, veteris: old, former, 2

1 **locūtōribus**: an IL coin-word. *-tor* is a common suffix which denotes the agent.
2 **(quōmodo) neglegant**: continuing the indir. quest. from the previous pg.
quī... teneat aut doceat: *whoever observes or teaches*; pr. conditional with a relative (A&G 519)
4 **sī... dīxerit...** : 3 s. fut. pf. act. indic. in an implied future condition (A&G 516)
ut... displiceat: 3 s. pr. act. subj. prim. seq. result clause
magis... quam...
5 **ōderit**: *odisse* pf. system, pr. meanings.
cum sit: conc. *cum* cl. (A&G 549)
6 **quasi... sentiat... (quasi)... vastet**: **quasi** along with the other comparative particles usually takes the subj. (A&G 524)
perniciosius... quam... gravius quam... interior... quam: comparatives with **quam**
7 **quō**: abl. of cause
8 **persequendō... inimīcandō**: *by persecuting... being hostile*; abl. s. n. gerunds of manner
litterārum: obj. gen. with **scientia**
10 **sē facere id alterī**: acc./inf. in indir. state. implied by **scrīpta cōnscientia**

sēcrētus es, habitāns in excelsīs in silentiō, deus sōlus magnus, lēge īnfatīgābilī spargēns poenālēs caecitātēs suprā inlicitās cupiditātēs, cum homō ēloquentiae fāmam quaeritāns ante hominem iūdicem circumstante hominum multitūdine inimīcum suum odiō immānissimō īnsectāns vigilantissimē cavet, nē per linguae errōrem dīcat, 'inter hominibus', et nē per mentis furōrem hominem auferat ex hominibus, nōn cavet.

1.19.30 hōrum ego puer mōrum in līmine iacēbam miser, et huius harēnae palaestra erat illa, ubi magis timēbam barbarismum facere quam cavēbam, sī facerem, nōn facientibus invidēre. Dīcō

---

auferō, -ferre, abstulī, ablātum: carry away
barbarismus, -ī m.: an impropriety of speech, barbarism, 2
caecitās, -tātis f.: blindness, 1
caveō, -ēre: be on one's guard, beware, 3
circumstō, -āre, -stetī: stand around, 1
cupiditās, -tātis f.: desire, eagerness, 3
ēloquentia, -ae f.: eloquence, 2
excellō, -ere, -, excelsus: excel, 2
fāma, -ae f.: rumor, reputation, report, 1
furor, -ōris m.: madness, frenzy, rage, 1
habitō (1): live, dwell, 1
harēna (arēna), -ae f.: sand, *arena*, 1
iaceō, -ēre, iacuī: lie (down), 2
immānis, -e: immense, huge, 2
īnfatīgābilis, -e: indefatigable, 1
inimīcus, -a, -um: unfriendly, 2
inlicitus, -a, -um: unlawful, illicit, 1
īnsector, -ārī, īnsectātus: attack, hound, 1
inter: between, among (acc.), 4
invideō, -ēre, -vīdī, -vīsum: envy, hate, 1
iūdex, iūdicis m.: judge, juror, 2
līmen, līminis n.: threshold, 2
lingua, ae f.: tongue, language, 4
mēns, mentis f.: mind, intent, purpose, 3
mōs, mōris m.: custom, way; character, 3
multitūdō, -tūdinis f.: multitude, 1
odium, -iī n.: hatred, 2
palaestra, -ae f.: palaestra (wrestling arena), 1
poenālis, -e: of punishment, 3
quaeritō (1): seek, search for, 1
sēcrētus, -a, -um: secret, hidden away, distant; *subst.* the esoteric, a secret, 4
silentium, -iī n.: silence, 1
sōlus, -a, -um: alone, only, lone, sole, 3
spargō, -ere, sparsī, sparsum: sprinkle, 1
suprā: above, over (and beyond), on the top, 2
timeō, -ēre, -uī: fear, be afraid of, 2
vigilō (1): be awake, be vigilant, 2

11 **ēloquentiae fāmam:** apposit. gen. (A&G 343d), a variation of subj. gen.

13 **quaeritāns:** *ever seeking*; the addition of -*itō*, -*tō*, or *sō* to a stem (as here to *quaer-*) makes it iterative (A&G 263.2), but these verbs often replaced the original verbs in meaning and usage (e.g., *cantāre* for *cānere*)
hominem iūdicem: *judging human* or *human judge*; the use of nouns as adjs. is not normal in CL, but becomes more so in IL (C&M 64). Arts takes *human* as emphasized as opposed to *divine.*

15 **cavet, nē... dīcat... nē... auferat... nōn cavet**: *cavēre* usually takes *ut* + subj. in CL (A&G 563d) but see below.

19 **timēbam... facere**: generally verbs of fearing (*timēre, metuere, verēri*) take the fear cl. in CL (A&G 564), but the compl. inf. is sometimes found and becomes widespread in IL (Arts 98-99)

20 **cavēbam... facientibus invidēre**: perhaps to parallel **timēbam facere**; **facientibus** is dat. with special verb (A&G 367)
cavēbam sī facerem: past gen. cond. (A&G 514.D.2b)

haec et cōnfiteor tibi, deus meus, in quibus laudābar ab eīs quibus placēre tunc mihi erat honestē vīvere. nōn enim vidēbam vorāginem turpitūdinis in quam prōiectus eram ab oculīs tuīs. nam in illīs iam quid mē foedius fuit, ubi etiam tālibus displicēbam fallendō innumerābilibus mendāciīs et paedagōgum et magistrōs et parentēs amōre lūdendī, studiō spectandī nūgātōria et imitandī lūdicra inquiētūdine? fūrta etiam faciēbam dē cellāriō parentum et dē mēnsā, vel gulā imperitante vel ut habērem quod darem puerīs lūdum suum mihi quō pariter ūtique dēlectābantur tamen vendentibus. in quō etiam lūdō fraudulentās victōriās ipse vānā

---

amor, amōris m.: love, 4
cellārium, -iī n.: store-room, pantry, 1
displiceō, -ere, -uī: displease, 2
foedus, -a, -um: ugly, foul, filthy
fraudulentus, -a, -um: deceitful, 1
fūrtum, -ī n.: theft, 1
gula, -ae f.: throat, gullet, 1
honestus, -a, -um: respectable, honorable, 2
imitor, -ārī, imitātum: imitate, copy, 4
imperitō (1): command, 1
innumerābilis, -e: innumerable, 1
inquiētūdō, -inis f.: restlessness, 1
lūdicrum, -ī n.: amusement; sport, 1
lūdus, -ī m.: game, sport; school, 4
mendācium, -ī n.: lie, 1
mēnsa, -ae f.: table, 1
nūgātōrius, -a, -um: trifling, worthless, 1
paedagōgus, -ī m.: tutor, 2
pār, paris: equal, similar, even; peer, 2
placeō, -ēre, -uī, placitum: please, be pleasing, pf. part. subst.: something agreed upon, prescription, principle, 3
prōiciō, -icere, -iēcī, -iectum: throw forth, 2
spectō (1): watch, look at, 2
studium, -ī n.: zeal, desire, pursuit, 2
turpitūdō, -inis f.: disgrace, turpitude, 3
vendō, -ere, vendidī, vendītus: sell, 1
victōria, -ae f.: victory, 2
vorāgō, -inis f.: chasm, abyss, 1

21 **placēre (eīs) erat mihi honestē vīvere**: **placēre** and **vīvere** are subj. and pred. infs.
22 **nōn vidēbam**: *I was not recognizing*
mē foedius: *fouler than I*; abl. of compar.
23 **prōiectus eram**: 1 sg. m. plpf. pass. ind.
tālibus (hominibus): dat. with special verbs (A&G 367)
24 **in illīs (quae et cōnfiteor)**
25 **fallendō... paedagōgum et magistrōs et parentēs**: abl. n. sg. gerund of means with a dir. obj. To take a dir. obj. a gerund often assimilates the gen. and num. of its object. But as we've seen, A. is inconsistent (A&G 503a note 1; cf. G&L 427 note 3). Cf. p. 4 l. 6; p. 17 l. 12.
26 **amōre lūdendī, studiō spectandī... imitandī** : causal abls. and obj. gens.
nūgātōria... ludicra: dir. objs. of gerund ; see above.
27 **inquiētūdine**: abl. of manner usually has **cum** unless modified by an adj. but not necessarily in poetry and IL (A&G 412 and n.); it is possible that **lūdrica** actually modifies **inquiētūdine** but the parallelism with **spectandī nūgātōria** seems stronger.
fūrta faciēbam : *I stole...*
28 **vel gulā imperitante**: s. abl. abs. pr. act. part. integrated into the sentence structure (A&G 419b; C&M 84c)
puerīs vendentibus lūdum suum mihi...
29 **ut habērem**: 1 sg. impf. act. subj. sec. seq. in purp. cl.
quod darem: 1 sg. impf. act. subj., sec. seq., in rel. cl. of char. (A&G 535a)

excellentiae cupiditāte victus saepe aucupābar. quid autem tam nōlēbam patī atque atrōciter, sī dēprehenderem, arguēbam, quam id quod aliīs faciēbam? et, sī dēprehēnsus arguerer, saevīre magis quam cēdere libēbat. istane est innocentia puerīlis? nōn est, domine, nōn est. ōrō tē, deus meus: nam haec ipsa sunt quae ā paedagōgīs et magistrīs, ā nucibus et pilulīs et passeribus, ad praefectōs et rēgēs, aurum, praedia, mancipia, haec ipsa omnīnō succēdentibus maiōribus aetātibus trānseunt, sīcuti ferulīs maiōra supplicia succēdunt. humilitātis ergō signum in statūrā pueritiae, rēx noster, probāstī, cum aīstī, 'tālium est rēgnum caelōrum.'

---

aiō: say, 2
arguō, -ere, -uī: declare; accuse, 2
atrōx (atrōcis): terrible, fierce, cruel, 1
aucupor (1): chase, hunt, lie in wait for, 1
aurum, -ī n.: gold, 1
cēdō, -ere, cessī, cessus: withdraw, move, 1
cupiditās, -tātis f.: desire, eagerness, *lust,* 3
dēprehendō, -ere, -dī, -ēnsus: seize, catch, 3
excellō, -ere, -, excelsus: excel, 2
ferula, -ae f.: reed, whip, rod, 2
humilitās, -ātis f.: lowness, 2
innocentia, -ae f.: innocence, 2
libet, libuit: it is pleasing (impers.), 2
mancipium, -ī n.: property, slave, 1
nux, nucis f.: nut, 1
omnīnō: altogether, (strengthens neg.) *at all*, 4
ōrō (1): plead, beg, pray, 2
paedagōgus, -ī m.: tutor, 2
passer, passeris m.: sparrow
patior, -ī, passus: suffer, endure; allow, 4
pilula, -ae f.: a little ball, 1
praedium, -iī n.: estate, 1
praeficiō -ere -fēcī: put in charge over, 1
probō (1): approve, commend, 2
puerīlis, -e: boyish, childish
pueritia, -ae, f.: childhood, 4
rēx, rēgis m.: king; *adj*. ruling, royal, 4
rēgnum, -ī n.: kingdom, realm, power
rēx, rēgis m.: king; *adj*. ruling, royal, 4
saepe: often
saeviō, -īre, -iī: rage, be savage
sīcut(i): just as as, so as, 4
statūra, -ae f.: height, stature
succēdō, -ere, -cessī: follow (on), (dat.), 4
supplicium, -iī n.: punishment, 1
tam: so, so much, so very, such, 2
vincō, -ere, vīcī, victum: conquer, overcome, defeat, 2

vanā.. cupiditāte: abl. of means
excellentiae: obj. gen. with words of feeling (A&G 348)

2 **(quid) atrōciter, sī dēprehenderem arguēbam:** past gen. cond. (A&G 514.D.2b)

3 **saevīre libēbat (mihi) magis quam cēdere:** *to rage was more pleasing (to me) than to yield*; *libet* often takes the dat. and inf. (A&G 208c)

4 **ista** = *haec*

5 **ōrō tē**: "a parenthetic formula of reverence intended here to soften the dictatorial vehemence of the [foregoing] statement" (G&M)

8 **ad praefectōs... succēdentibus:** again acc. and dat. set parallel syntactically ; **succēdentibus** is a subst. that takes the dat. **aetātibus** as its object (A&G 370)

9 **signum**: *symbol.*

10 **aīstī**: 2 sg. pf. act. indic.; like *inquam* **aiō** is used parenthetically but unlike *inquam* not exclusively so (see a dict.). The pf. formation of *aiō* is an IL construction.

1.20.31 sed tamen, domine, tibi excellentissimō atque optimō conditōrī et rēctōrī ūniversitātis, deō nostrō grātiās, etiamsī mē puerum tantum esse voluissēs. eram enim etiam tunc, vīvēbam atque sentiēbam meamque incolumitātem, vestīgium sēcrētissimae ūnitātis ex quā eram, cūrae habēbam, custōdiēbam interiōre sēnsū integritātem sēnsuum meōrum inque ipsīs parvīs parvārumque rērum cōgitātiōnibus vēritāte dēlectābar. fallī nōlēbam, memoriā vigēbam, locūtiōne īnstruēbar, amīcitiā mulcēbar, fugiēbam dolōrem, abiectiōnem, ignōrantiam. quid in tālī animante nōn mīrābile atque laudābile? at ista omnia deī meī dōna sunt. nōn mihi

---

abiectiō, -ōnis f.: rejecting, throwing away, 1
amīcitia, -ae, f.: friendship, 2
animō (1): enliven, animate, 2
at: but; mind you; but, you say, 4
cōgitātio, -tiōnis f.: thought, reflection, 2
conditor, -toris m.: founder, 1
cūra, -ae f.: care, concern, worry, 1
custōdiō, -īre, -īvī, -ītum: guard, preserve, 1
dolor, -ōris m.: grief, pain, 4
dōnum, -ī n.: gift, 2
etiamsī: even if, 3
excellēns, -entis: surpassing, superb, 1
fugiō, -ere, fūgī: flee, escape, 2
grātia, -ae f.: gratitude; favor, thanks, 3
ignōrantia, -ae f. : ignorance, 1
incolumitās, -ātis f.: security, safety, 2
īnstruō, -ere, -strūxī: equip, draw up, 2
integritās, -tātis f.: wholeness, integrity, 1
interior, -ius: inner, interior, 2
laudābilis, -e: worthy of praise, laudable, 3
locūtiō, -iōnis f.: speech, discourse, 1
memoria, -ae f.: memory, 4
mīrābilis, -e: amazing, wonderful ,1
mulceō, -ēre, -sī, mulsus: soothe, calm, 1
optimus, -a, -um: best, noblest, finest, 2
rēctor, -ōris m.: director; ruler, 1
sēcrētus, -a, -um: secret, hidden away, distant; *subst.* the esoteric, a secret, 4
tantus, -a, -um: so great, so much, so large, 3
ūnitās, -ātis f.: unity, 1
ūniversitās, -ātis f.: the whole, entirety, 2
vēritās, -tātis f.: truth, 4
vestīgium, -iī n.: track, foot-print, trace, 3
vigeō, -ēre: be strong/vigorous, thrive, 1

12 **ūniversitātis:** obj. gen.
tibi… deō nostrō grātiās (agō):
etiamsī… voluissēs: protasis of past or mixed CTF, for which is the apodosis is an implied, *et tamen bonus fuissēs* or *essēs*
13 **eram:** existential *sum*
14 **meamque incolumintātem… cūrae (mihi) habēbam** : *my safety I had for a care for myself*; implied double dative construction, suppressed to avoid pleonasm.
vestīgium sēcrētissimae ūnitātis ex quā eram : "Here again the turn of thought is Neo-Platonic" (G&M).
15 **(et) custōdiēbam**: asyndeton.
interiōre sēnsū: abl. of means; "I suppose… that this inner sense not only perceives what it gets from the five bodily senses, but also that they themselves are perceived by it" (G&M)
17 **vēritāte** *dēlectābar*: in the pass. takes an abl. of means, but may here, like *fruor* or *utor* be being used in a middle sense, e.g., *I delighted myself in them* (C&M 77)
fallī: pr. pass. compl. inf. with **nōlēbam** (A&G 456)
memoriā: abl. of respect
locūtiōne… amīcitiā: abls. of means
19 **in tālī animante**: *in one thus ensouled* or *thus minded*: **animante** is subst.
20 **ista** = *haec* ; **deī meī**: subj. gen.

ego dedī haec, et bona sunt, et haec omnia ego. bonus ergō est quī fēcit mē, et ipse est bonum meum, et illī exultō bonīs omnibus quibus etiam puer eram. hoc enim peccābam, quod nōn in ipsō sed in creātūrīs eius mē atque cēterīs voluptātēs, sublīmitātēs, vēritātēs quaerēbam, atque ita inruēbam in dolōrēs, cōnfūsiōnēs, errōrēs. grātiās tibi, dulcēdō mea et honor meus et fīdūcia mea, deus meus, grātiās tibi dē dōnīs tuīs: sed tū mihi ea servā. ita enim servābis mē, et augēbuntur et perficientur quae dedistī mihi, et erō ipse tēcum, quia et ut sim tū dedistī mihi.

---

augeō, -ēre, auxī, auctum: increase, enrich
cēterī, -ae, -a: the other, remaining
cōnfūsiō, -ōnis f.: mixing, blending
creātūra, -ae f.: creation, creature, 3
dolor, -ōris m.: grief, pain, 4
dōnum, -ī n.: gift, 2
dulcēdō, -inis f.: sweetness, 3
exultō (exsultō) (1): be ecstatic, exult
fīdūcia, -ae f.: confidence, reliance, trust
grātia, -ae f.: gratitude; favor, thanks, 3
honor, -ōris m.: honor, glory; offering, 3
inruō, -ere, -ruī: rush in
perficiō, -ere, -fēcī, -fectum: accomplish, 2
servō (1): save, keep, preserve, 2
sublīmitās, -ātis f.: height, loftiness
vēritās, -tātis f.: truth, 4
voluptās, -tātis f.: pleasure, delight

21 **et haec omnia ego**: *and all these things constitute my "self"*; compare Lord Tennyson's "Ulysses": "I am a part of all that I have met, // yet experience is an arch wherethru..."
ego: By use of the pronoun (without the verb), he emphasizes the idea of selfhood and personality, but *vice versa* to emphasize the sheer fact of existence (for the idea p. 7 of Gildersleeve's *Problems in Greek Syntax*). The reader might compare now p. 3, *non enim ego iam inferi.*
22: **illī**: ethical dat. *for his sake*
exultō bonīs omnibus: **exultō** takes the bare abl. of cause (A&G 404a)
23 **quibus**: *in virtue of which*; abl. of cause
peccābam : "It is indeed necessary that someone looking to the beauty in bodies not rush headlong with them, but, fully aware that they are images and traces and shadows, flee to that whose images they are" Plotinus, *Enneads* (G&M)
mē...cēterīs: apposition to **creaturīs**
24 **volutptātēs** *etc.*: here one may again note the increased frequency of abstract subst. in IL (C&M 57)
26 **(agō) grātiās tibi... grātiās tibi**:
27 **dē dōnīs tuīs**: abl. of source (A&G 403)
servābis... augēbuntur... perficientur... erō...: all futures that look forward to the very end of the *Confessions*, which famously ends in 3 open-ended futures: *accipietur, sic invenietur, sic aperietur.*
28 **erō** : 1st s. fut. of *sum, esse*
29 **et ut sim tū dedistī**: *even that I exist you gave to me*; verbs of permitting can take either *ut* + subj. or inf. (A&G 563c). See above note on **ego.**

Latin Text

For Classroom Use

1.1.1 magnus es, domine, et laudābilis valdē. magna virtūs tua et sapientiae tuae nōn est numerus. et laudāre tē vult homō, aliqua portiō creātūrae tuae, et homō circumferēns mortālitātem suam, circumferēns testimōnium peccātī suī et testimōnium quia superbīs resistis; et tamen laudāre tē vult homō, aliqua portiō creātūrae tuae. tū excitās ut laudāre tē dēlectet, quia fēcistī nōs ad tē et inquiētum est cor nostrum dōnec requiēscat in tē. dā mihi, domine, scīre et intellegere utrum sit prius invocāre tē an laudāre tē, et scīre tē prius sit an invocāre tē. sed quis tē invocat nesciēns tē? aliud enim prō aliō potest invocāre nesciēns. an potius invocāris ut sciāris? quōmodo autem invocābunt, in quem nōn crēdidērunt? aut quōmodo crēdent sine praedicante? et laudābunt dominum quī requīrunt eum: quaerentēs enim inveniunt eum et invenientēs laudābunt eum. quaeram tē, domine, invocāns tē et invocem tē crēdēns in tē: praedicātus enim es nōbīs. invocat tē, domine, fidēs mea, quam dedistī mihi, quam īnspīrāstī mihi per hūmānitātem fīliī tuī, per ministerium praedicātōris tuī.

1.2.2 et quōmodo invocābō deum meum, deum et dominum meum, quoniam utique in mē ipsum eum vocābō, cum invocābō eum? et quis locus est in mē quō veniat in mē deus meus, quō deus veniat in mē, deus quī fēcit caelum et terram? itane, domine deus meus? est quicquam in mē quod capiat tē? an vērō caelum et terra, quae fēcistī et in quibus mē fēcistī, capiunt tē? an quia sine tē nōn esset quidquid est, fit ut quidquid est capiat tē? quoniam itaque et ego sum, quid petō ut veniās in mē, quī nōn essem nisi essēs in mē? nōn enim ego iam īnferī, et tamen etiam ibi es, nam etsī dēscenderō in īnfernum, ades. nōn ergō essem, deus meus, nōn omnīnō essem, nisi essēs in mē. an potius nōn essem nisi essem in tē, ex quō omnia, per quem omnia, in quō omnia? etiam sīc, domine, etiam sīc. quō tē invocō, cum in tē sim? aut unde veniās in mē? quō enim recēdam extrā caelum et terram, ut inde in mē veniat deus meus, quī dīxit, ‘caelum et terram ego impleō’?

1.3.3 capiunt ergōne tē caelum et terra, quoniam tū implēs ea? an implēs et restat, quoniam nōn tē capiunt? et quō refundis quidquid implētō caelō et terrā restat ex tē? an nōn opus habēs ut quōquam contineāris, quī continēs omnia, quoniam quae implēs continendō implēs? nōn enim vāsa quae tē plēna sunt stabilem tē faciunt, quia etsī frangantur nōn effunderis. et cum effunderis super nōs, nōn tū iacēs sed ērigis nōs, nec tū dissipāris sed conligis nōs. sed quae implēs omnia, tē tōtō implēs omnia. an quia nōn possunt tē tōtum capere omnia, partem tuī capiunt et eandem partem simul omnia capiunt? an singulās singula et maiōrēs maiōra, minōrēs minōra capiunt? ergō est aliqua pars tua maior, aliqua minor? an ubīque tōtus es et rēs nūlla tē tōtum capit?

1.4.4 quid es ergō, deus meus? quid, rogō, nisi dominus deus? quis enim dominus praeter dominum? aut quis deus praeter deum nostrum? summe, optime, potentissime, omnipotentissime, misericordissīme et iūstissime, sēcrētissime et praesentissime, pulcherrime et fortissime, stabilīs et incomprehēnsibilīs, immūtābilīs mūtāns omnia, numquam novus numquam vetus, innovāns omnia et in vetustātem perdūcēns superbōs et nesciunt. semper agēns semper quiētus, conligēns et nōn egēns, portāns et implēns et prōtegēns, creāns et nūtriēns et perficiēns, quaerēns cum nihil dēsit tibi. amās nec aestuās, zēlās et sēcūrus es, paenitet tē et nōn dolēs, īrāsceris et tranquillus es, opera mūtās nec mūtās cōnsilium, recipis quod invenīs et numquam āmīsistī. numquam inops et gaudēs lucrīs, numquam avārus et ūsūrās exigis, superērogātur tibi ut dēbeās: et quis habet quicquam nōn tuum? reddis dēbita nūllī dēbēns, dōnās dēbita nihil perdēns. et quid dīximus, deus meus, vīta mea, dulcēdō mea sāncta, aut quid dīcit aliquis cum dē tē dīcit? et vae tacentibus dē tē, quoniam loquācēs mūtī sunt.

1.5.5 quis mihi dabit adquiēscere in tē? quis dabit mihi ut veniās in cor meum et inēbriēs illud, ut oblīvīscar mala mea et ūnum bonum meum amplectar, tē? quid mihi es? miserēre ut loquar. quid tibi sum ipse, ut amārī tē iubeās ā mē et, nisi faciam, īrāscāris mihi et minēris ingentēs miseriās? parvane ipsa est sī nōn amem tē? eī mihi! dīc mihi per miserātiōnēs tuās, domine deus meus, quid sīs mihi. dīc animae meae, 'salūs tua ego sum': sīc dīc ut audiam. ecce aurēs cordis meī ante tē, domine. aperī eās et dīc animae meae, 'salūs tua ego sum.' curram post vōcem hanc et apprehendam tē. nōlī abscondere ā mē faciem tuam: moriar, nē moriar, ut eam videam.

1.5.6 angusta est domus animae meae quō veniās ad eam: dīlātētur abs tē. ruīnōsa est: refice eam. habet quae offendant oculōs tuōs: fateor et sciō. sed quis mundābit eam? aut cui alterī praeter tē clāmābō, 'ab occultīs meīs mundā mē, domine, et ab aliēnīs parce servō tuō?' crēdō, propter quod et loquor, domine: tū scīs. nōnne tibi prōlocūtus sum adversum mē dēlicta mea, deus meus, et tū dīmīsistī impietātem cordis meī? nōn iūdiciō contendō tēcum, quī vēritās es, et ego nōlō fallere mē ipsum, nē mentiātur inīquitās mea sibi. nōn ergō iūdiciō contendō tēcum, quia, sī inīquitātēs observāverīs, domine, domine, quis sustinēbit?

1.6.7 sed tamen sine mē loquī apud misericordiam tuam, mē terram et cinerem sine tamen loquī. quoniam ecce misericordia tua est, nōn homō, inrīsor meus, cui loquor. et tū fortasse inrīdēs mē, sed conversus miserēberis meī. quid enim est quod volō dīcere, domine, nisi quia nesciō unde vēnerim hūc, in istam dīcō vītam mortālem an mortem vītālem? nesciō. et suscēpērunt mē cōnsōlātiōnēs miserātiōnum tuārum, sīcut audīvī ā parentibus carnis meae, ex quō et in quā mē fōrmāstī in tempore: nōn enim ego meminī. excēpērunt ergō mē cōnsōlātiōnēs lactis hūmānī, nec māter mea vel nūtrīcēs meae sibi ūbera implēbant, sed tū mihi per eās dabās alimentum īnfantiae secundum īnstitūtiōnem tuam et dīvitiās usque ad fundum rērum dispositās. tū etiam mihi dabās nōlle amplius quam dabās, et nūtrientibus mē dare mihi velle quod eīs dabās: dare enim mihi per ōrdinātum affectum volēbant quō abundābant ex tē. nam bonum erat eīs bonum meum ex eīs, quod ex eīs nōn sed per eās erat. ex tē quippe bona omnia, deus, et ex deō meō salūs mihi ūniversa. quod animadvertī postmodum, clāmante tē mihi per haec ipsa quae tribuis intus et foris. nam tunc sūgere nōram et adquiēscere dēlectātiōnibus, flēre autem offēnsiōnēs carnis meae, nihil amplius.

1.6.8 post et rīdēre coepī, dormiēns prīmō, deinde vigilāns. hoc enim dē mē mihi indicātum est et crēdidī, quoniam sīc vidēmus aliōs īnfantēs: nam ista mea nōn meminī. et ecce paulātim sentiēbam ubi essem, et voluntātēs meās volēbam ostendere eīs per quōs implērentur, et nōn poteram, quia illae intus erant, foris autem illī, nec ūllō suō sēnsū valēbant introīre in animam meam. itaque iactābam membra et vōcēs, signa similia voluntātibus meīs, pauca quae poteram, quālia poteram: nōn enim erant vērē similia. et cum mihi nōn obtemperābātur, vel nōn intellēctō vel nē obesset, indignābar nōn subditīs maiōribus et līberīs nōn servientibus, et mē dē illīs flendō vindicābam. tālēs esse īnfantēs didicī quōs discere potuī, et mē tālem fuisse magis mihi ipsī indicāvērunt nescientēs quam scientēs nūtrītōrēs meī.

1.6.9 et ecce īnfantia mea ōlim mortua est et ego vīvō. tū autem, domine, quī et semper vīvis et nihil moritur in tē, quoniam ante prīmōrdia saeculōrum, et ante omne quod vel ante dīcī potest, tū es, et deus es dominusque omnium quae creāstī, et apud tē rērum omnium īnstabilium stant causae, et rērum omnium mūtābilium immūtābilēs manent orīginēs, et omnium inratiōnālium et temporālium sempiternae vīvunt ratiōnēs, dīc mihi supplicī tuō, deus, et misericors miserō tuō dīc mihi, utrum alicui iam aetātī meae mortuae successerit īnfantia mea. an illa est quam ēgī intrā vīscera mātris meae? nam et dē illā mihi nōnnihil indicātum est et praegnantēs ipse vīdī fēminās. quid ante hanc etiam, dulcēdō mea, deus meus? fuīne alicubi aut aliquis? nam quis mihi dicat ista, nōn habeō; nec pater nec māter potuērunt, nec aliōrum experīmentum nec memoria mea. an inrīdēs mē ista quaerentem tēque dē hōc quod novī laudārī ā mē iubēs et cōnfitērī mē tibi?

1.6.10 cōnfiteor tibi, domine caelī et terrae, laudem dīcēns tibi dē prīmōrdiīs et īnfantiā meā, quae nōn meminī. et dedistī eā hominī ex aliīs dē sē conicere et auctōritātibus etiam mulierculārum multa dē sē crēdere. eram enim et vīvēbam etiam tunc, et signa quibus sēnsa mea nōta aliīs facerem iam in fīne īnfantiae quaerēbam. unde hoc tāle animal nisi abs tē, domine? an quisquam sē faciendī erit artifex? aut ūlla vēna trahitur aliunde quā esse et vīvere currat in nōs, praeterquam quod tū facis nōs, domine, cui esse et vīvere nōn aliud atque aliud, quia summē esse ac summē vīvere idipsum est? summus enim es et nōn mūtāris, neque peragitur in tē hodiernus diēs, et tamen in tē peragitur, quia in tē sunt et ista omnia: nōn enim habērent viās trānseundī, nisi continērēs eās. et quoniam annī tuī nōn dēficiunt, annī tuī hodiernus diēs. et quam multī iam diēs nostrī et patrum nostrōrum per hodiernum tuum trānsiērunt et ex illō accēpērunt modōs et utcumque extitērunt, et trānsībunt adhūc aliī et accipient et utcumque existent. tū autem īdem ipse es et omnia crāstina atque ultrā omniaque hesterna et retrō hodiē faciēs, hodiē fēcistī. quid ad mē, sī quis nōn intellegat? gaudeat et ipse dīcēns, 'quid est hoc?' gaudeat etiam sīc, et amet nōn inveniendō invenīre potius quam inveniendō nōn invenīre tē.

1.7.11 exaudī, deus. vae peccātīs hominum! et homō dīcit haec, et miserēris eius, quoniam tū fēcistī eum et peccātum nōn fēcistī in eō. quis mē commemorat peccātum īnfantiae meae, quoniam nēmō mundus ā peccātō cōram tē, nec īnfāns cuius est ūnīus diēī vīta super terram? quis mē commemorat? an quīlibet tantillus nunc parvulus, in quō videō quod nōn meminī dē mē? quid ergō tunc peccābam? an quia ūberibus inhiābam plōrāns? nam sī nunc faciam, nōn quidem ūberibus sed ēscae congruentī annīs meīs ita inhiāns, dērīdēbor atque reprehendar iūstissimē. tunc ergō reprehendenda faciēbam, sed quia reprehendentem intellegere nōn poteram, nec mōs reprehendī mē nec ratiō sinēbat: nam extirpāmus et ēicimus ista crēscentēs. nec vīdī quemquam scientem, cum aliquid pūrgat, bona prōicere. an prō tempore etiam illa bona erant, flendō petere etiam quod noxiē darētur, indignārī ācriter nōn subiectīs hominibus līberīs et maiōribus hīsque, ā quibus genitus est, multīsque praetereā prūdentiōribus nōn ad nūtum voluntātis obtemperantibus feriendō nocēre nītī quantum potest, quia nōn oboedītur imperiīs quibus perniciōsē oboedīrētur? ita inbēcillitās membrōrum īnfantīlium innocēns est, nōn animus īnfantium. Vīdī ego et expertus sum zēlantem parvulum: nōndum loquēbātur et intuēbātur pallidus amārō aspectū conlactāneum suum. quis hoc ignōrat? expiāre sē dīcunt ista mātrēs atque nūtrīcēs nesciō quibus remediīs. nisi vērō et ista innocentia est, in fonte lactis ūbertim mānante atque abundante opis egentissimum et illō adhūc ūnō alimentō vītam dūcentem cōnsortem nōn patī. sed blandē tolerantur haec, nōn quia nūlla vel parva, sed quia aetātis accessū peritūra sunt. quod licet probēs, cum ferrī aequō animō eādem ipsa nōn possunt quandō in aliquō annōsiōre dēprehenduntur.

1.7.12 tū itaque, domine deus meus, quī dedistī vītam īnfantī et corpus, quod ita, ut vidēmus, īnstrūxistī sēnsibus, compēgistī membrīs, figūrā decorāstī prōque eius ūniversitāte atque incolumitāte omnēs cōnātūs animantīs īnsinuāstī, iubēs mē laudāre tē in istīs et cōnfitērī tibi et psallere nōminī tuō, altissimē, quia deus es omnipotēns et bonus, etiamsī sōla ista fēcissēs, quae nēmō alius potest facere nisi tū, ūne, ā quō est omnis modus, fōrmōsissimē, quī fōrmās omnia et lēge tuā ōrdinās omnia. hanc ergō aetātem, domine, quam mē vīxisse nōn meminī, dē quā aliīs crēdidī et quam mē ēgisse ex aliīs īnfantibus coniēcī, quamquam ista multum fīda coniectūra sit, piget mē adnumerāre huic vītae meae quam vīvō in hōc saeculō. quantum enim attinet ad oblīviōnis meae tenebrās, pār illī est quam vīxī in mātris uterō. quod sī et in inīquitāte conceptus sum et in peccātīs māter mea mē in uterō aluit, ubi, ōrō tē, deus meus, ubi, domine, ego, servus tuus, ubi aut quandō innocēns fuī? sed ecce omittō illud tempus: et quid mihi iam cum eō est, cuius nūlla vestīgia recōlō?

1.8.13 nōnne ab īnfantiā hūc pergēns venī in pueritiam? vel potius ipsa in mē vēnit et successit īnfantiae? nec discessit illa: quō enim abiit? et tamen iam nōn erat. nōn enim eram īnfāns quī nōn fārer, sed iam puer loquēns eram. et meminī hoc, et unde loquī didiceram post advertī. nōn enim docēbant mē maiōrēs hominēs, praebentēs mihi verba certō aliquō ōrdine doctrīnae sīcut paulō post litterās, sed ego ipse mente quam dedistī mihi, deus meus, cum gemitibus et vōcibus variīs et variīs membrōrum mōtibus edere vellem sēnsa cordis meī, ut voluntātī parerētur, nec valērem quae volēbam omnia nec quibus volēbam omnibus, prēnsābam memoriā. cum ipsī appellābant rem aliquam et cum secundum eam vōcem corpus ad aliquid movēbant, vidēbam et tenēbam hoc ab eīs vocārī rem illam quod sonābant cum eam vellent ostendere. hoc autem eōs velle ex mōtū corporis aperiēbātur tamquam verbīs nātūrālibus omnium gentium, quae fīunt vultū et nūtū oculōrum cēterōrumque membrōrum āctū et sonitū vōcis indicante affectiōnem animī in petendīs, habendīs, reiciendīs fugiendīsve rēbus. ita verba in variīs sententiīs locīs suīs posita et crēbrō audīta quārum rērum signa essent paulātim conligēbam meāsque iam voluntātēs ēdomitō in eīs signīs ōre per haec ēnūntiābam. sīc cum hīs inter quōs eram voluntātum ēnūntiandārum signa commūnicāvī, et vītae hūmānae procellōsam societātem altius ingressūs sum, pendēns ex parentum auctōritāte nūtūque maiōrum hominum.

1.9.14 deus, deus meus, quās ibi miseriās expertus sum et lūdificātiōnēs, quandōquidem rēctē mihi vīvere puerō id prōpōnēbātur, obtemperāre monentibus, ut in hōc saeculō flōrērem et excellerem linguōsīs artibus ad honōrem hominum et falsās dīvitiās famulantibus. inde in scholam datus sum ut discerem litterās, in quibus quid ūtilitātis esset ignōrābam miser. et tamen, sī sēgnis in discendō essem, vāpulābam. laudābātur enim hoc ā maiōribus, et multī ante nōs vītam istam agentēs praestrūxerant aerumnōsās viās, per quās trānsīre cōgēbāmur multiplicātō labōre et dolōre fīliīs Adam. invenīmus autem, domine, hominēs rogantēs tē et didicimus ab eīs, sentientēs tē, ut poterāmus, esse magnum aliquem quī possēs etiam nōn appārēns sēnsibus nostrīs exaudīre nōs et subvenīre nōbīs. nam puer coepī rogāre tē, auxilium et refugium meum, et in tuam invocātiōnem rumpēbam nōdōs linguae meae et rogābam tē parvus nōn parvō affectū, nē in scholā vāpulārem. et cum mē nōn exaudiēbās, quod nōn erat ad īnsipientiam mihi, rīdēbantur ā maiōribus hominibus usque ab ipsīs parentibus, quī mihi accidere malī nihil volēbant, plāgae meae, magnum tunc et grave malum meum.

1.9.15 estne quisquam, domine, tam magnus animus, praegrandī affectū tibi cohaerēns, estne, inquam, quisquam (facit enim hoc quaedam etiam stoliditās: est ergō), quī tibi piē cohaerendō ita sit affectus granditer, ut eculeōs et ungulās atque huiuscemodī varia tormenta (prō quibus effugiendīs tibi per ūniversās terrās cum timōre magnō supplicātur) ita parvī aestimet, dīligēns eōs quī haec acerbissimē formīdant, quemadmodum parentēs nostrī rīdēbant tormenta quibus puerī ā magistrīs afflīgēbāmur? nōn enim aut minus ea metuēbāmus aut minus tē dē hīs ēvādendīs dēprecābāmur, et peccābāmus tamen minus scrībendō aut legendō aut cōgitandō dē litterīs quam exigēbātur ā nōbīs. nōn enim dēerat, domine, memoria vel ingenium, quae nōs habēre voluistī prō illā aetāte satis, sed dēlectābat lūdere et vindicābātur in nōs ab eīs quī tālia utique agēbant. sed maiōrum nūgae negōtia vocantur, puerōrum autem tālia cum sint, pūniuntur ā maiōribus, et nēmō miserātur puerōs vel illōs vel utrōsque. nisi vērō approbat quisquam bonus rērum arbiter vāpulāsse mē, quia lūdēbam pilā puer et eō lūdō impediēbar quōminus celeriter discerem litterās, quibus maior dēfōrmius lūderem. aut aliud faciēbat īdem ipse ā quō vāpulābam, quī sī in aliquā quaestiunculā ā condoctōre suō victus esset, magis bīle atque invidiā torquērētur quam ego, cum in certāmine pilae ā conlūsōre meō superābar?

1.10.16 et tamen peccābam, domine deus, ōrdinātor et creātor rērum omnium nātūrālium, peccātōrum autem tantum ōrdinātor, domine deus meus, peccābam faciendō contrā praecepta parentum et magistrōrum illōrum. poteram enim posteā bene ūtī litterīs, quās volēbant ut discerem quōcumque animō illī meī. nōn enim meliōra ēligēns inoboediēns eram, sed amōre lūdendī, amāns in certāminibus superbās victōriās et scalpī aurēs meās falsīs fābellīs, quō prūrīrent ārdentius, eādem cūriōsitāte magis magisque per oculōs ēmicante in spectācula, lūdōs maiōrum -- quōs tamen quī edunt, eā dignitāte praeditī excellunt, ut hoc paene omnēs optent parvulīs suīs, quōs tamen caedī libenter patiuntur, sī spectāculīs tālibus impediantur ab studiō quō eōs ad tālia edenda cupiunt pervenīre. vidē ista, domine, misericorditer, et līberā nōs iam invocantēs tē, līberā etiam eōs quī nōndum tē invocant, ut invocent tē et līberēs eōs.

1.11.17 audieram enim ego adhūc puer dē vītā aeternā prōmissā nōbīs per humilitātem dominī deī nostrī dēscendentis ad superbiam nostram, et signābar iam signō crucis eius, et condiēbar eius sale iam inde ab uterō mātris meae, quae multum spērāvit in tē. vīdistī, domine, cum adhūc puer essem et quōdam diē pressū stomachī repente aestuārem paene moritūrus, vīdistī, deus meus, quoniam cūstōs meus iam erās, quō mōtū animī et quā fidē baptismum Chrīstī tuī, deī et dominī meī, flāgitāvī ā pietāte mātris meae et mātris omnium nostrum, ecclēsiae tuae. et conturbāta māter carnis meae, quoniam et sempiternam salūtem meam cārius parturiēbat corde castō in fidē tuā, iam cūrāret festīnābunda ut sacrāmentīs salūtāribus initiārer et abluerer, tē, domine Iēsu, cōnfitēns in remissiōnem peccātōrum, nisi statim recreātus essem. dīlāta est itaque mundātiō mea, quasi necesse esset ut adhūc sordidārer sī vīverem, quia vidēlicet post lavācrum illud maior et perīculōsior in sordibus dēlictōrum reātus foret. ita iam crēdēbam et illa et omnis domus, nisi pater sōlus, quī tamen nōn ēvīcit in mē iūs māternae pietātis, quōminus in Chrīstum crēderem, sīcut ille nōndum crēdiderat. nam illa satagēbat ut tū mihi pater essēs, deus meus, potius quam ille, et in hōc adiuvābās eam, ut superāret virum, cui melior serviēbat, quia et in hōc tibi ūtique id iubentī serviēbat.

1.11.18 rogō tē, deus meus: vellem scīre, sī tū etiam vellēs, quō cōnsiliō dilātus sum nē tunc baptīzārer, utrum bonō meō mihi quasi laxāta sint lōra peccandī. an nōn laxāta sunt? unde ergō etiam nunc dē aliīs atque aliīs sonat undique in auribus nostrīs: ‘sine illum, faciat: nōndum enim baptīzātus est’? et tamen in salūte corporis nōn dīcimus: ‘sine vulnerētur amplius: nōndum enim sānātus est.’ quantō ergō melius et cito sānārer et id agerētur mēcum meōrum meāque dīligentiā, ut recepta salūs animae meae tūta esset tūtēlā tuā, quī dedissēs eam. melius vērō. sed quot et quantī flūctūs impendere temptātiōnum post pueritiam vidēbantur, nōverat eōs iam illa māter et terram per eōs, unde posteā fōrmārer, quam ipsam iam effigiem committere volēbat.

1.12.19 in ipsā tamen pueritiā, dē quā mihi minus quam dē adulēscentiā metuēbātur, nōn amābam litterās et mē in eās urgērī ōderam, et urgēbar tamen et bene mihi fīēbat. nec faciēbam ego bene (nōn enim discerem nisi cōgerer; nēmō autem invītus bene facit, etiamsī bonum est quod facit), nec quī mē urgēbant bene faciēbant, sed bene mihi fīēbat abs tē, deus meus. illī enim nōn intuēbantur quō referrem quod mē discere cōgēbant, praeterquam ad satiandās īnsatiābilēs cupiditātēs cōpiōsae inopiae et ignōminiōsae glōriae. tū vērō, cui numerātī sunt capillī nostrī, errōre omnium quī mihi īnstābant ut discerem ūtēbāris ad ūtilitātem meam, meō autem, quī discere nōlēbam, ūtēbāris ad poenam meam, quā plectī nōn eram indignus, tantillus puer et tantus peccātor. ita dē nōn bene facientibus tū bene faciēbās mihi et dē peccante mē ipsō iūstē retribuēbās mihi. iussistī enim et sīc est, ut poena sua sibi sit omnis inōrdinātus animus.

1.13.20 quid autem erat causae cūr Graecās litterās ōderam, quibus puerulus imbuēbar? nē nunc quidem mihi satis explōrātum est. adamāveram enim latīnās, nōn quās prīmī magistrī sed quās docent quī grammaticī vocantur. nam illās prīmās, ubi legere et scrībere et numerāre discitur, nōn minus onerōsās poenālēsque habēbam quam omnēs Graecās. unde tamen et hoc nisi dē peccātō et vānitāte vītae, quā cārō eram et spīritus ambulāns et nōn revertēns? nam ūtique meliōrēs, quia certiōrēs, erant prīmae illae litterae quibus fīēbat in mē et factum est et habeō illud ut et legam, sī quid scrīptum inveniō, et scrībam ipse, sī quid volō, quam illae quibus tenēre cōgēbar Aenēae nesciō cuius errōrēs, oblītus errōrum meōrum, et plōrāre Dīdōnem mortuam, quia sē occīdit ab amōre, cum intereā mē ipsum in hīs ā tē morientem, deus, vīta mea, siccīs oculīs ferrem miserrimus.

1.13.21 quid enim miserius miserō nōn miserante sē ipsum et flente Dīdōnis mortem, quae fīēbat āmandō Aenēān, nōn flente autem mortem suam, quae fīēbat nōn āmandō tē, deus, lūmen cordis meī et pānis ōris intus animae meae et virtūs marītāns mentem meam et sinum cōgitātiōnis meae? nōn tē amābam, et fornicābar abs tē, et fornicantī sonābat undique: 'eugē! eugē!' amīcitia enim mundī huius fornicātiō est abs tē et 'eugē! eugē!' dīcitur ut pudeat, sī nōn ita homō sit. et haec nōn flēbam, et flēbam Dīdōnem extīnctam ferrōque extrēmā secūtam, sequēns ipse extrēma condita tua relictō tē et terra iēns in terram. et sī prohibērer ea legere, dolērem, quia nōn legerem quod dolērem. tālī dēmentiā honestiōrēs et ūberiōrēs litterae putantur quam illae quibus legere et scrībere didicī.

1.13.22 sed nunc in animā meā clāmet deus meus, et vēritās tua dicat mihi, 'nōn est ita, nōn est ita.' melior est prōrsus doctrīna illa prior. nam ecce parātior sum oblīvīscī errōrēs Aenēae atque omnia eius modī quam scrībere et legere. at enim vēla pendent līminibus grammaticārum scholārum, sed nōn illa magis honōrem sēcrētī quam tegimentum errōris significant. nōn clāment adversus mē quōs iam nōn timeō, dum cōnfiteor tibi quae vult anima mea, deus meus, et adquiēscō in reprehēnsiōne malārum viārum meārum, ut dīligam bonās viās tuās, nōn clāment adversus mē venditōrēs grammaticae vel ēmptōrēs, quia, sī prōpōnam eīs interrogāns, utrum vērum sit quod Aenēān aliquandō Carthāginem vēnisse poēta dīcit, indoctiōrēs nescīre sē respondēbunt, doctiōrēs autem etiam negābunt vērum esse. at sī quaeram quibus litterīs scrībātur Aenēae nōmen, omnēs mihi quī haec didicērunt vērum respondent secundum id pactum et placitum quō inter sē hominēs ista signa firmārunt. item sī quaeram quid hōrum maiōre vītae huius incommodō quisque oblīvīscātur, legere et scrībere an poētica illa figmenta, quis nōn videat quid respōnsūrus sit, quī nōn est penitus oblītus suī? peccābam ergō puer cum illa inānia istīs ūtiliōribus amōre praepōnēbam, vel potius ista ōderam, illa amābam. iam vērō ūnum et ūnum duo, duo et duo quattuor, odiōsa cantiō mihi erat, et dulcissimum spectāculum vānitātis, equus ligneus plēnus armātīs et Troiae incendium atque ipsīus umbra Creūsae.

1.14.23 cūr ergō Graecam etiam grammaticam ōderam tālia cantantem? nam et Homērus perītus texere tālēs fābellās et dulcissimē vānus est, mihi tamen amārus erat puerō. crēdō etiam Graecīs puerīs Vergilius ita sit, cum eum sīc discere cōguntur ut ego illum. vidēlicet difficultās, difficultās omnīnō ēdiscendae linguae peregrīnae, quasi felle aspergēbat omnēs suāvitātēs Graecās fābulōsārum nārrātiōnum. nūlla enim verba illa nōveram, et saevīs terrōribus ac poenīs ut nōssem īnstābātur mihi vehementer. nam et latīna aliquandō īnfāns ūtique nūlla nōveram, et tamen advertendō didicī sine ūllō metū atque cruciātū, inter etiam blandīmenta nūtrīcum et ioca adrīdentium et laetitiās adlūdentium. didicī vērō illa sine poenālī onere urgentium, cum mē urgēret cor meum ad parienda concepta sua, quae nōn possem, nisi aliqua verba didicissem nōn ā docentibus sed ā loquentibus, in quōrum et ego auribus parturiēbam quidquid sentiēbam. hinc satis ēlūcet maiōrem habēre vim ad discendā ista līberam cūriōsitātem quam meticulōsam necessitātem. sed illīus flūxum haec restringit lēgibus tuīs, deus, lēgibus tuīs ā magistrōrum ferulīs usque ad temptātiōnēs martyrum, valentibus lēgibus tuīs miscēre salūbrēs amāritūdinēs revocantēs nōs ad tē ā iūcunditāte pestiferā quā recessimus ā tē.

1.15.24 exaudī, domine, dēprecātiōnem meam, nē dēficiat anima mea sub disciplīnā tuā neque dēficiam in cōnfitendō tibi miserātiōnēs tuās, quibus ēruistī mē ab omnibus viīs meīs pessimīs, ut dulcēscās mihi super omnēs sēductiōnēs quās sequēbar, et amem tē validissimē, et amplexer manum tuam tōtīs praecordiīs meīs, et ēruās mē ab omnī temptātiōne usque in fīnem. ecce enim tū, domine, rēx meus et deus meus, tibi serviat quidquid ūtile puer didicī, tibi serviat quod loquor et scrībō et lēgō et numerō, quoniam cum vāna discerem tū disciplīnam dabās mihi, et in eīs vānīs peccāta dēlectātiōnum meārum dīmīsistī mihi. didicī enim in eīs multa verba ūtilia, sed et in rēbus nōn vānīs discī possunt, et ea via tūta est in quā puerī ambulārent.

1.16.25 sed vae tibi, flūmen mōris hūmānī! quis resistet tibi? quamdiū nōn siccāberis? quousque volvēs Ēvae fīliōs in mare magnum et formīdulōsum, quod vix trānseunt quī lignum cōnscenderint? nōnne ego in tē lēgī et tonantem Iovem et adulterantem? et ūtique nōn posset haec duo, sed āctum est ut habēret auctōritātem ad imitandum vērum adulterium lēnōcinante falsō tonitrū. quis autem paenulātōrum magistrōrum audit aure sōbriā ex eōdem pulvere hominem clāmantem et dīcentem: 'fingēbat haec Homērus et hūmāna ad deōs trānsferēbat: dīvīna māllem ad nōs'? sed vērius dīcitur quod fingēbat haec quidem ille, sed hominibus flāgitiōsīs dīvīna tribuendō, nē flāgitia flāgitia putārentur et ut, quisquis ea fēcisset, nōn hominēs perditōs sed caelestēs deōs vidērētur imitātus.

1.16.26 et tamen, ō flūmen Tartareum, iactantur in tē fīliī hominum cum mercēdibus, ut haec discant, et magna rēs agitur cum hōc agitur pūblicē in forō, in cōnspectū lēgum suprā mercēdem salāria dēcernentium, et saxa tua percutis et sonās dīcēns: 'hinc verba discuntur, hinc adquīritur ēloquentia, rēbus persuādendīs sententiīsque explicandīs maximē necessāria.' ita vērō nōn cognōscerēmus verba haec, 'imbrem aureum' et 'gremium' et 'fūcum' et 'templa caelī' et alia verba quae in eō locō scrīpta sunt, nisi Terentius indūceret nēquam adulēscentem prōpōnentem sibi Iovem ad exemplum stuprī, dum spectat tabulam quandam pictam in pariete ubi inerat pictūra haec, Iovem quō pactō Danaē mīsisse aiunt in gremium quondam imbrem aureum, fūcum factum mulierī? et vidē quemadmodum sē concitat ad libīdinem quasi caelestī magisteriō: 'at quem deum! inquit quī templa caelī summō sonitū concutit. ego homunciō id nōn facerem? ego vērō illud fēcī ac libēns.' nōn omnīnō per hanc turpitūdinem verba ista commodius discuntur, sed per haec verba turpitūdō ista cōnfīdentius perpetrātur. nōn accūsō verba quasi vāsa ēlēcta atque pretiōsa, sed vīnum errōris quod in eīs nōbīs propīnābātur ab ēbriīs doctōribus, et nisi biberēmus caedēbāmur, nec appellāre ad aliquem iūdicem sōbrium licēbat. et tamen ego, deus meus, in cuius cōnspectū iam sēcūra est recordātiō mea, libenter haec didicī, et eīs dēlectābar miser, et ob hōc bonae speī puer appellābar.

1.17.27 sine mē, deus meus, dīcere aliquid et dē ingeniō meō, mūnere tuō, in quibus ā mē dēlīrāmentīs atterēbātur. prōpōnēbātur enim mihi negōtium, animae meae satis inquiētum praemiō laudis et dēdecoris vel plāgārum metū, ut dīcerem verba Iūnōnis īrāscentis et dolentis quod nōn posset Ītaliā Teucrōrum āvertere rēgem, quae numquam Iūnōnem dīxisse audieram. Sed figmentōrum poēticōrum vestīgia errantēs sequī cōgēbāmur, et tāle aliquid dīcere solūtīs verbīs quāle poēta dīxisset versibus. et ille dīcēbat laudābilius in quō prō dignitāte adumbrātae persōnae īrae ac dolōris similior affectus ēminēbat, verbīs sententiās congruenter vestientibus. ut quid mihi illud, ō vēra vīta, deus meus, quod mihi recitantī adclāmābātur prae multīs coaetāneīs et conlēctōribus meīs? nōnne ecce illa omnia fūmus et ventus? itane aliud nōn erat ubi exercērētur ingenium et lingua mea? laudēs tuae, domine, laudēs tuae per scrīptūrās tuās suspenderent palmitem cordis meī, et nōn raperētur per inānia nūgārum turpis praeda volātilibus. Nōn enim ūnō modo sacrificātur trānsgressōribus angelīs.

1.18.28 quid autem mīrum, quod in vānitātēs ita ferēbar et ā tē, deus meus, ībam forās, quandō mihi imitandī prōpōnēbantur hominēs quī aliqua facta sua nōn mala, sī cum barbarismō aut soloecismō ēnūntiārent, reprehēnsī cōnfundēbantur, sī autem libīdinēs suās integrīs et rīte cōnsequentibus verbīs cōpiōsē ōrnātēque narrārent, laudātī glōriābantur? vidēs haec, domine, et tacēs, longanimis et multum misericors et vērāx. numquid semper tacēbis? et nunc ēruīs dē hōc immānissimō profundō quaererentem tē animam et sitientem dēlectātiōnēs tuās, et cuius cor dīcit tibi, ‘quaesīvī vultum tuum.’ vultum tuum, domine, requīram: nam longē ā vultū tuō in affectū tenebrōsō. nōn enim pedibus aut ā spatiīs locōrum ītur abs tē aut redītur ad tē, aut vērō fīlius ille tuus minor equōs vel currūs vel nāvēs quaesīvit, aut āvolāvit pinnā vīsibilī, aut mōtō poplite iter ēgit, ut in longinquā regiōne vīvēns prōdige dissipāret quod dederās proficīscentī, dulcis pater quia dederās, et egēnō redeuntī dulcior: in affectū ergō libīdinōsō, id enim est tenebrōsō, atque id est longē ā vultū tuō.

1.18.29 vidē, domine deus, et patienter, ut vidēs, vidē quōmodo dīligenter observent fīliī hominum pacta litterārum et syllabārum accepta ā priōribus locūtōribus, et ā tē accepta aeterna pacta perpetuae salūtis neglegant, ut quī illa sonōrum vetera placita teneat aut doceat, sī contrā disciplīnam grammaticam sine adspīrātiōne prīmae syllabae hominem dīxerit, magis displiceat hominibus quam sī contrā tua praecepta hominem ōderit, cum sit homō. quasi vērō quemlibet inimīcum hominem perniciōsius sentiat quam ipsum odium quō in eum inrītātur, aut vastet quisquam persequendō alium gravius quam cor suum vastat inimīcandō. et certē nōn est interior litterārum scientia quam scrīpta cōnscientia, id sē alterī facere quod nōlit patī. quam tū sēcrētus es, habitāns in excelsīs in silentiō, deus sōlus magnus, lēge īnfatīgābilī spargēns poenālēs caecitātēs suprā inlicitās cupiditātēs, cum homō ēloquentiae fāmam quaeritāns ante hominem iūdicem circumstante hominum multitūdine inimīcum suum odiō immānissimō īnsectāns vigilantissimē cavet, nē per linguae errōrem dīcat, 'inter hominibus', et nē per mentis furōrem hominem auferat ex hominibus, nōn cavet.

1.19.30 hōrum ego puer mōrum in līmine iacēbam miser, et huius harēnae palaestra erat illa, ubi magis timēbam barbarismum facere quam cavēbam, sī facerem, nōn facientibus invidēre. Dīcō haec et cōnfiteor tibi, deus meus, in quibus laudābar ab eīs quibus placēre tunc mihi erat honestē vīvere. nōn enim vidēbam vorāginem turpitūdinis in quam prōiectus eram ab oculīs tuīs. nam in illīs iam quid mē foedius fuit, ubi etiam tālibus displicēbam fallendō innumerābilibus mendāciīs et paedagōgum et magistrōs et parentēs amōre lūdendī, studiō spectandī nūgātōria et imitandī lūdicra inquiētūdine? fūrta etiam faciēbam dē cellāriō parentum et dē mēnsā, vel gulā imperitante vel ut habērem quod darem puerīs lūdum suum mihi quō pariter ūtique dēlectābantur tamen vendentibus. in quō etiam lūdō fraudulentās victōriās ipse vānā excellentiae cupiditāte victus saepe aucupābar. quid autem tam nōlēbam patī atque atrōciter, sī dēprehenderem, arguēbam, quam id quod aliīs faciēbam? et, sī dēprehēnsus arguerer, saevīre magis quam cēdere libēbat. istane est innocentia puerīlis? nōn est, domine, nōn est. ōrō tē, deus meus: nam haec ipsa sunt quae ā paedagōgīs et magistrīs, ā nucibus et pilulīs et passeribus, ad praefectōs et rēgēs, aurum, praedia, mancipia, haec ipsa omnīnō succēdentibus maiōribus aetātibus trānseunt, sīcuti ferulīs maiōra supplicia succēdunt. humilitātis ergō signum in statūrā pueritiae, rēx noster, probāstī, cum aīstī, 'tālium est rēgnum caelōrum.'

1.20.31 sed tamen, domine, tibi excellentissimō atque optimō conditōrī et rēctōrī ūniversitātis, deō nostrō grātiās, etiamsī mē puerum tantum esse voluissēs. eram enim etiam tunc, vīvēbam atque sentiēbam meamque incolumitātem, vestīgium sēcrētissimae ūnitātis ex quā eram, cūrae habēbam, custōdiēbam interiōre sēnsū integritātem sēnsuum meōrum inque ipsīs parvīs parvārumque rērum cōgitātiōnibus vēritāte dēlectābar. fallī nōlēbam, memoriā vigēbam, locūtiōne īnstruēbar, amīcitiā mulcēbar, fugiēbam dolōrem, abiectiōnem, ignōrantiam. quid in tālī animante nōn mīrābile atque laudābile? at ista omnia deī meī dōna sunt. nōn mihi ego dedī haec, et bona sunt, et haec omnia ego. bonus ergō est quī fēcit mē, et ipse est bonum meum, et illī exultō bonīs omnibus quibus etiam puer eram. hoc enim peccābam, quod nōn in ipsō sed in creātūrīs eius mē atque cēterīs voluptātēs, sublīmitātēs, vēritātēs quaerēbam, atque ita inruēbam in dolōrēs, cōnfūsiōnēs, errōrēs. grātiās tibi, dulcēdō mea et honor meus et fīdūcia mea, deus meus, grātiās tibi dē dōnīs tuīs: sed tū mihi ea servā. ita enim servābis mē, et augēbuntur et perficientur quae dedistī mihi, et erō ipse tēcum, quia et ut sim tū dedistī mihi.

ALPHABETIZED CORE VOCABULARY
CONFESSIONS BOOK I

ā, ab, abs: (away) from, out of; by
ad: to, toward
adhūc: thus, to this point, still; even, just
Aenēās, -ae m.: Aeneas
aetās, aetātis f.: age, lifetime, time
affectus, -ūs m.: affection, feeling
agō, -ere, ēgī, āctum: drive, do, spend, lead (a life)
aliquis, aliquid (quī, quid): anyone, anything; some, any
alius, -a, -ud: other, another, else
amō (): love, like
an: or (in questions)
anima, -ae f.: breath, spirit, soul
animus, -ī m: soul, will; minī; intention
ante: before, in front of (acc.)
atque (=ac): and, and also, and even
audiō, -īre, -īvī, audītum: hear, listen to
auris, auris f.: ear
aut: or (aut...aut – either…or)
autem: however, but; moreover
bene: well
bonus, -a, -um: good, noble, kind
caelum, -ī n.: sky, heaven
capiō, -ere, cēpī, captum: take, seize, hold, contain
clāmō (): shout, cry out
cōgō, -ere, -ēgī, coactum: compel
cōnfiteor, -ērī, -fessum: admit, reveal, confess (dat.)
cor, cordis n. hearT
crēdō, -ere, -didī, creditum: believe, trust (+dat.)
cum: with (abl.); when, since, although,
dē: down from, from, about, concerning (abl)
dēlectō (): delight (compl. inf.), please, in pass. + abl.
deus, -ī m.: god, divinity, deity
dīcō, -ere, dīxī, dictus: say, speak, tell
diēs, -ēī m./f.: day, time, season
discō, -ere, didicī: learn, come to know, get acquainted with (acc.)
dō, dare, dedī, datum: give; grant
dominus, -ī m.: master, lord
ē, ex: out from, from, out of (+ abl.)
ecce: behold, look
ego, mihi, mē, mē: I
enim: for, indeed, in truth
ergō: therefore
error errōris m.: wandering, error
et: and; also, even
etiam: also, even; besides

ALPHABETIZED CORE VOCABULARY
CONFESSIONS BOOK I

faciō, -ere, fēcī, factum: do, make
fallō, -ere, fefellī, falsum: deceive
fīlius, -iī m.: son
fiō, fierī, factus sum: become, be made, happen (+ ut and subj.)
fleō, -ēre, -ēvī, flētum: weep, cry, bewail (acc.)
Graecus, -a, -um: Greek
grammaticus, -a, -um.: of grammar, grammatical; *m. subst.* grammarian, teacher of the second level of education in the Roman world, after students had learned their ABC's
habeō, -ēre, habuī, -itus: have, hold; consider
hic, haec, hoc: this, these
homō, -inis m./f.: man, mortal, human
iam: now, already; + nōn, no longer
īdem, eadem, idem: the same
ille, illa, illud: that, those
impleō, -ēre, -ēvī: fill; fulfill, complete
in: in (+ abl.) , into (acc.)
īnfāns, -fantis m. f.: infant
īnfantia, -ae f.: inability to speak, infancy
inveniō, -īre, -vēnī: come upon, find
invocō (): call on, pray to, invoke
ipse, ipsa, ipsum: -self; the very
is, ea, id: this, that; he, she, it
iste, ista, istud: this/these *or* that/those
ita: so, thus
iubeō, iubēre, iussī, iussum: order
laudō (): praise, glorify
legō, -ere, lēgī, lectum: read, choose
lēx, lēgis f.: law, regulation, decree
littera, -ae f.: letter (of the alphabet); pl. literature, epistle
loquor, loquī, locūtus sum: speak, address
lūdō, -ere, lūsī, lūsus: play; play with
magis: more, rather
magister, magistrī m.: teacher
magnus, -a, -um: great, large; important
maior, māius: greater; older; ancestors
malus, -a, -um: bad, evil
māter, mātris f.: mother
melior, melius: better
membrum, -ī n.: limb, member
meminī, -isse: remember; recall
meus, -a, -um: my, mine
minor, minus: less, smaller; *adv.* less
miser, -a, -um: sad, miserable, gloomy
modus, -ī m.: way, manner; limit; just, only

morior, morī, mortuus sum: die
multus, -a, -um: much, many
nam: for, because
ne: (introduces a yes/no question)
nē: lest, that not, no, not
nec: and not (nec…nec: neither…nor)
nesciō, -īre, -scīvī, -scītum: not know
nihil: nothing
nisi: if not, unless, except
nōlō, nōlle, nōluī: not wish, be unwilling
nōn: not
nōndum: not yet
nōs, nōbīs: we, us
noster, nostra, nostrum: our
nūllus, -a, -um: none, no, no one
numquam: never, at no time
nunc: now, at present
oblīvīscor, -ī, -lītus sum: forget (acc. or gen.)
oculus, -ī, m.: eye
ōdī, -isse: hate
omnis, omne: every, all
parēns, -rentis m.: parent, ancestor
parvus, -a, -um: small, little
pater, patris, m.: father
peccātum, -ī n.: sin, offense
peccō (): sin, commit an offense
per: through, over, across (acc)
possum, posse, potuī: be able, can, avail
post: after, behind (acc.), in A., toward; afterward
potius: rather, preferably (comp. of potis 'possible')
prīmus -a -um: first
prō: before, for, in behalf of; in accordance with (abl.),
prōpōnō, -ere, -suī, -situm: put or set forth
puer, puerī, m.: boy
quaerō, -ere, quaesīvī: search for, ask
quam: than, as; how
quasi: as if
que: and
quī, quae, quod (quis? quid?): who, which, that
quia: because, that
quisquam, quidquam (quicquam): anyone, anything
quisquis, quidquid: whoever, whatever
quoniam: since now, seeing that
reprehendō, -ere, -dī: blame; hold back; scold
rēs, reī, f.: thing, matter, affair; pl. reality, the universe

ALPHABETIZED CORE VOCABULARY CONFESSIONS BOOK I

rogō (): ask
salūs, -ūtis f.: safety, refuge; health; salvation
sciō, -īre, -īvī (iī), -ītus: know (how + inf.)
scrībō, -ere, scrīpsī, scrīptum: write
sē, sibi: himself, her-, it-, them-
sed: but
sēnsus, -ūs m.: feeling, perception, sensation
sentiō, -īre, sēnsī, sēnsum: feel, perceive
serviō, -īre, -īvī, -ītum: be slave to, serve, (dat.)
sī: if
sīc: thus, in this way
signum, -ī n.: sign, signal; symbol
sine: without (abl.)
sum, esse, fuī, futūrum: be
summus, -a, -um: highest, greatest, top of
suus, -a, -um: his, her, its, their (own)
tālis, -e: of such a sort
tamen: nevertheless, however, anyway
terra, -ae. f.: earth, ground, land; pl. the earth
tōtus -a, -um: whole, entire
trānseō, -īre, -iī (īvī), itus: pass (by)
tū: you
tunc: then, at that time
tuus, -a, -um: your, yours
ubi: where, when
unde: from where, whence
ūnus, -a, -um: one
urgeō, -ere, ursī: press, urge, distress
ut: as, just as, when (+ ind.); (so) that, in order that
utique: in any case, by all means, certainly
vānus, -a, -um: worthless; vain, futile, false
vel: or, either…or (inclusive)
veniō, -īre, vēnī, ventus: come, go
verbum, -ī n.: word, speech
vērō: in truth, in fact, certainly
vērus, -a, -um: true, real
via, -ae, f.: way, road, street
videō, vidēre, vīdī, vīsum: see
vīta, -ae, f.: life
vīvō, -ere, vīxī, vīctum: live
volō, velle, voluī: will, wish, be willing, (compl. inf.)
voluntās, -tātis f.: will, wish, desire
vōx, vōcis, f.: sound, voice; word, utterance, quotation
vultus, -ūs m.: expression, countenance, face

Dictionary of Grammatical and Rhetorical Terms[1]

Ablative [*ab-* away, *latus-* carried]: the Latin case denoting 'carrying away from', i.e., separation.
Absolute [*ab-* away, *solut-* loosed] : when a noun or part. is used apart (loosed from) the other grammatical elements of the sentence or clause.
Abstract [*ab-* away, *stract-* drawn] : a noun which is taken out of (drawn away from) concrete circumstances, such as a principle or sim., e.g., love, faith.
Accent [*ad-* to, *cantus-* song]: higher stress (whether pitch or volume) laid on a syllable.
Accusative [*ad-* to, *c(a)usa-* assign, attribute, charge] : a case (noun ending) which indicates the direct object of the verb, but often also indepently or w/ prepositions associated with (A) motion toward and, regarding time, (B) duration.
Active Voice [*act-* do,, cause, make, act] : a voice of the verb (opp. to mid. and pass.) which usually views the subjective as the agent, *dealing* not *feeling* the action.
Adjective [*ad-* to, *jact-* thrown, put] : a word *put to* or *up against*, and so modifying, a noun.
Adverb [*ad-* to, *verbum-* word, verb] : a word closely connected to or modifying a verb.
Affix [*ad-* to, *fixum-* attached]: a syllable or letter attached to the end of a word.
Agreement: said of nouns and verbs when their grammatical information matches in, depending on specific circumstances, case, number, or gender.
Anacolouthon [*an-* not, *acolouthon-* following] : a break later in a sentence from the grammatical order or sequence the earlier part leads the reader to expect.
Antecedent [*ante-* before, *cedent-* going]: the noun which *goes before* (at least in thought, if not in fact) the relative pronoun, which must agree w/ the pronoun in number and gender (not case)
Antithesis [*anti-* against, *thesis-* placing] : placing of one word against (next to) another, encouraging the reader to contrast them.
Apodosis [*apo-* back, *dosis-* giving] : the "then" or "therefore" clause of a condition, considered by the Greeks as a kind of debt to be paid when the condition of the "if" clause was fulfilled.
Apposition [*ad-* to, by *positum-* placed] : A word or phrase *placed beside* another word or phrase necessarily in the same case, but not in the same gender or number. The word(s) so placed is called an Appositive. Generally its purpose is explanation or expansion of the preceding idea.
Article [*articulus-* a little joint or limb] : used in Greek to denote a little word united several words together, used in Eng. to mean "the" and "a".[2]
Aspirate [*ad-* to, *spiratum-* breathed] : an accentuated breathing at the start of a word, marked in English by "H", which causes certain changes of form (in Greek).
Asyndeton [*a-* not, *syndeton-* bound together]: a lack of conjunctions with the effect of speed, urgency, or abruptness.
Auxiliary Verb [*auxilia-* to help]: verbs that are used as helpers or companions to other verbs, as forms of "be" and "have" in Eng.
Bathos [*bathos-* depth]: a fall "to the pits" from a serious or elevated height to the humorous or absurd.
Case [*casus* - falling, happening] : A way of marking the grammatical use of the noun (in a sentence or clause) by the ending it takes. the Nominitive was considered the primary form, from which all other case endings "fell away": see Decline.
Clause [*clausum-* shut (off/out)] : words or phrases *shut up* or *closed off* within limits. The limits are the (subordinating) conjunctions which precede (or follow) it.
Cognate Accusative [*cum-* together; *natus-* born]: an object that denotes something akin to the action of the verb.
Cognate Accusative [*cum-* together; *natus-* born]: an

[1] Adapted from E.A. Abbot's "How to Parse" in the Public Domain and expanded.
[2] Ibid. "foolishly introduced into English…"

object that denotes something akin to the action of the verb.
Comparative Degree : form of an adjective which denotes that a greater degree of a quality exists in one thing than another.
Complementary Infinitive [*cum-* togethe; *pleo-* fill]: an infinitive which *fills up* the meaning *together with* the verb it belongs to, often necessary for the sense of the sentence e.g., *I decided to go to the store*. This is a sub-group of the Object Infinitve.
Conative [*conari-* attempt]: describes a use of the (usually) imperfect times or sometimes a particular root-stem which emphasizes the action as being "attempted" or tried, often repeatedly.
Conjunction [*cum-* together; *iungo-* join]: a word that *joins* two sentences *together*.
Copula [*copula-* bond]: verbs of being and seeming and many verbs in the passive, because they *bind* the subject and the predicate in Logic (equate the one to the other).
Correlative [*cum-* together; *re-* back, again; *latus*-carried]: words which, in referring to one another, divide a sentence or clause into two or more parts being compared as related, e.g., *both Cicero and Caesar thought highly of themselves;* or *as Cicero loved himself so also Caesar.*
Dative [*dativus-* related to giving]: a Case ending which denotes the person to or for whom a thing is *given, granted,* etc. The most basic sense of the Dative is reference, functioning like an arrow it points to the person or thing for whom the action of the verb is of interest.
Declension [*de-* down; *clino-* tilt, bend]: The changing or "bending" all other case-endings of a noun from the Nominative, which was considered the "upright" standard from which the others "descended" or "bent away." See **Case** and **Noun**.
Denominative Verb [*de-* from; *nomen* -noun]: such verbs are those formed from the stems of nouns or adjectives or else made according to this pattern. Opp. to **Primitive Verbs**
Dentals [*dent-* tooth]: consonants pronounced with the aid of teeth, which in English are *n, d,* and *t.*
Dependent Clause [*de-* from; *pend-* hang]: = Subordinate Clause. A self-contained set of words or phrases which has its own subject and predicate but which nevertheless "hangs from" the main or independent clause logically, due to a conjunction which precedes the depenent clause.
Diphthong [*di-* two; *phthongos-* sound]: two vowel sounds pronounced together as one.
Direct Object : A noun or noun-equivalent (often a clause), which directly receives the action of the verb.
Ellipsis [*elleipsis-* omission]: The omission of words that are understood or implied in a sentence or clause, sometimes done for poetic effect and sometimes for brevity's sake; at other times it will merely reveal differences between languages and language-speakers.
Euphony [*eu-* well; *phonos-* sound]: Often used to describe changes in a language, conscious or not, which are done for the sake of "sounding well." A particularly prevalent feature of Greek morphology.
Foot : a discrete metrical unit or subunit of a poetic line or verse. In *Of man's / first dis / obedi / ence and / the fruit /* the words enclosed in slashes are *metrical feet* of Iambic *Penta*menter; likewise in *amaz / ing grace / how sweet / the sound*, which is the very popular Common Time or 4/3 with clear Iambics.
Frequentative Verb [*frequenter-* repeatedly]: a kind of verb that expressed a frequently repeated action, also called **Iterative.**
Fricatives [*frico-* to rub] : letters whose sounds are produced w/ constant friction, i.e, air blowing through: *f, s,* and *z*.
Gender [*genus-* class, kind]: a category used describe many nouns considerd to be of the same class; in Latin, Greek, and German one finds masculine, femine and neuter nouns, whereas in Spanish and Hebrew only masculine and femine, and in English none at all.
Genitive [*genitivus-* generating, having to do w/ source or kind] : name of the case denoting generation, origination and possession (and in Greek separation).

Gerund: a noun with verbal characterstics, i.e., a noun that shows action and can take objects and govern prepositional phrases. In English compare "*Running* to the store is fun for me" and "*Achieving* my goals is nice too."

Gutturals [*guttur-* throat]: The sounds made in the throat, which in English are *k* and the hard *g*.

Iambus: a metrical foot of two syllables. See **Foot**.

Idiom [*idios-* private, peculiar]: a form of expression unique to a language like the English "raining cats and dogs."

Imperative [*impero-* I command] : a mood of the verb which communicates a command, expressed in English by word position, "*get* me the remote control!"

Impersonal (Verb): Strictly of a verbal construction without a subject, emphasizing the action itself, *agitur* = it is going on, there is being done, common in Latin but not in English. Generally also used of those verbs like δεῖ in Greek or *licet* in Latin which do not occur in the first or second person, though they often have acc. subjs. or clauses and infinitives as their subjects.

Indicative [*indico-* I point out] : name of the mood of the verb which "points out" something in the world or fact, not feeling (compare **Subjunctive**).

Indirect Object: the noun or pronoun *to* or *for whom* (or *in whose interest*) an action is done. Most often represented by the Dative case, but also by prepositions.

Infinitive [*in-* not; *finitus-* limitedt] : the basic lexical form of the verb, which is sometimes considered a verbal noun (it is a dative in origin), but also sometimes a mood: in either case, important is that it is not *limited* by person or number.

Inflection [*inflectio-* a bending] : a bending of a word from its simple form by the means of word-endings, more broad than either conjugation or declension, and used to describe the whole set of phenomena together: hence we say that Latin is a more *inflected* language than English.

Interjection [*interiectio-* I a throwing in between, interruption] : an utterance *thrown between* other parts of speech to express emotion, e.g., *oh! alas!* etc.

Intransitive [*in-* not; *transitivus-* passing or crossing over, to] : a verb which does not take a direct object, i.e., which does not directly *pass through* or *across* an object.

Labials [*labium-* lip] : letters whose sounds are produced at the *lips* : *f, v, p, b, m*, and *w*.

Liquids [*liquidus-* flowing, fluid] : letters of flowing sound: *l* and *r*. These particularly effect the division of consonants in versification (see A&G 11)

Mood [*modus-* manner, mode] : the manner or moder in which a Verb expresses its action: as a wish or desire, or else varying degrees of reality (from certainty--Indicative--to vague supposition--Subjunctive)

Mute [*mutus-* silent] : letters pronounced by blocking entirely the passage of breath through the mouth before letting it through in a burst: *k, g, t(h), d, p(h), b,* and *c(h)*

Nasal [*nas-* nose] : letters whose sounds are produced by resonance in the nasal cavity: *n,* and *m*.

Nominative [*nomen-* name, noun] : the nominative *names* the subject; considered the basic or standard form of any given noun.

Noun [*nomen-* name, noun] : the <u>name</u> of any *person, place, thing, or idea.*

Object [*obiectum-* thrown against, in the way of] : the mark or goal of a verb or preposition: the place where the action of the verb terminates or has its end.

Objective Genitive: Said when the noun in the genitive is passive or the objective of the noun it modifies: Ex. For the love <u>of money</u> is the root of all kinds of evil…

Oblique Cases [*obliquus-* slanting] : cases other than the Nominative or Vocative.

Parenthesis [*para-* aside; *enthesis-* insertion] : a word, phrase or sentence *inserted on the side* of any sentence complete w/out it.

Participle [*particeps-* participating] : a form of a verb participating in the nature of a Verb *and* of an Adjective.

Partitive Genitive [*partitivus-* denoting participation in or partaking of] : a kind of genitive which denotes the class or group to which something belongs: one *of the sailors* died at sea.

Passive Voice [*passivus-* relating to suffering or experience] : the form of the verb in which the subject is said to *feel* the action of the verb rather than *deal* it out.

Palatals: letters produced by the palate, *g, k, ch,* and *y* (as in *you*).

Perfect Tense [*perfectum-* completed, finished] : name for a tense that depicts the action as finished or completed, in Latin both those done one time in the past, i.e., the simple past (Greek Aorist) and also those action done in the past but whose consequences last into the present (Greek Perfect), called the pregnant or present perfect.

Period [*periodos-* circle] : a sentence the whole of which makes a rounded path or full circle and whose sense is not completed until the very end.

Person : one of the important features of verbal inflection, whose options are 1st (I, we), 2nd (you, y'all), and 3rd (he/she/it, they).

Personification [*persona-* person; *ficatio-* making] : giving life and personality to something inanimate. As the beginning of Nietzsche's *Beyond Good and Evil*: "Now since we all know that Philosophy is a woman…"

Pluperfect [*plus-* more; *perfectum-* completed] : a tense which describes actions as *more completed* or *perfect* than the Perfect Tense: that is, prior to some other action already in the past.

Plural [*plur-* more, multiple] : one of two options (in Latin) for the number of nouns and verbs. Greek and Hebrew also has the Dual (decribing pairs of things or people).

Positive [*ponere-* to put (forward) or place] : the basic form of the adjective which presents (but does not compare) the quality.

Potential Subjuntive [*potens-* possible, powerful] : a type of subjunctive translated into English by *might, may* and *could,* which conceives of the action as possible or probable. In Greek the Optative takes this function.

Predicate [*praedicare-* proclaim, state] : a word or group of words making a statement about a Subject.

Preposition [*prae-* before; *positum-* placed] : an archaic adverb that fossilised in connection with certain cases and nouns, placed before the noun it modifies. The Prepositional Phrase is all that is governed by the preposition. Ex.: When *at the store* we bought cookies *for my mom.*

Primitive Verb : a verb forming its tense-stems directly from a root (i.e., not from a noun as a **Denominative Verb**)

Prodosis [*pro-* forth, forward; *dosis-* giving] : in a condition = the Protasis, i.e., the If- (*si* or εἰ/ἐάν) Clause, which sets up the condition to be fulfilled.

Pronoun [*pro-* for, instead of; *nomen-* noun] : a word that stands *in place of* its noun (its antecedent) which it matches in number and gender.

Protasis : = Prodosis.

Reflexive (Pronoun) [*re-* back(ward); *flect-* bend] : the noun or adjective that *bend back to* or reflects upon the subject of the sentence. Ex. While my friends got candy, *I* bought *myself* a watch.

Relative Pronoun [*re-* back; *latum-* carried] a name given to *who, which,* (and sometimes) *that*, when they *carry* one *back* to the Antecedent, whom they match in number and gender, but whose case is decided by the clause it is in.

Sibilant [*sibila-* hiss] : the unvoiced *s, sh*, and *z.*

Subjective Genitive: Said when the noun in the genitive is active or in possession of the word which it modifies: Ex. …the lust of the flesh, and the lust of the eyes…

Subordinate [*nomen-* name, noun] : the name of any *person, place, thing, or idea.*

Substantive: Functionally = a Noun, but it is generally used to describe an unusual Noun, whether an adjective acting as a noun or a clause.

Superlative [*super-* above; *latum-* carried] : the degree of the adjective which *carries* the quality *above* all others, e.g., best, greatest, lovliest.

Supplement [*sub-* up; *plere-* fill] : any part of speech, especialy a participle, which *fills up* the meaning of a verb.

Transitive [*transitivus-* passing or crossing over, to] : a verb which takes a direct object

Vocative [*vocare*- to call, address] : the case of direct address. Cf. the first line of the *Confessions*: Magnus es, <u>*domine*</u>, et laudabilis valde.

Made in the USA
Middletown, DE
09 August 2022

70927523R00066